ALBION GLORY

THE HIDDEN ARCHIVE UNCOVERED

ALBION GLORY
THE HIDDEN ARCHIVE UNCOVERED

Express & Star

breedon **books**
PUBLISHING

First published in Great Britain in 2001 by
The Breedon Books Publishing Company Limited
Breedon House, 3 The Parker Centre, Derby, DE21 4SZ.

ISBN 1 85983 243 1

Printed and bound by Butler & Tanner, Frome, Somerset
Jacket printing by GreenShires Ltd, Leicester

Contents

Acknowledgements 6

Introduction 7

Glorious Beginnings 8

In the Wembley Habit 10

Post-War Consolidation 18

Wembley Revisited 25

A Major Force 35

Sixties Rebuilding 45

When Albion Had the Mersey 'Beat' 63

Cup Specialists 73

Wembley Wonders 81

A Tough Act To Follow 94

Life in the Second 108

Up, Up and Away 123

Big Ron 134

Start of the Slide 157

Going Down 165

Super Bob! 175

Shoots of Recovery 183

Subscribers 187

Acknowledgements

It's gratifying to be able to pull together a book for Albion supporters that has had so much input from Albion supporters. And the reaction of those who have seen the content is enough to suggest we have come up with a worthy addition to the already substantial volumes of Hawthorns-related literature.

We would particularly like to thank Laurie Rampling and Tony Matthews for their kind provision of several dozen of the photos contained within these pages and for their encouragement along the way. Likewise, for supplying more modern stock, the efforts of Kevin Grice are much appreciated.

John Homer and Glenn Willmore, two men who need little introduction to Albion supporters, have spent many hours in their role as quality historians, helping us put captions to the pictures. So, too, Tony Matthews.

We must also say thank-you to other providers of pictures, such as Terry Wills, Barry Swash, Dean Walton, Mick Stanley, Dave Hewitt, Joyce and Trevor Brennan and Ian Smallman, who we regrettably omitted from the acknowledgements at the front of Albion Memories. And to folk like Pat and John Jordan for pointing us in the right direction in our pursuit.

It being an *Express & Star* production, the photographs of our Hawthorns lensmen, in particular Geoff Wright from the past and Paul Turner from the present, are very much to the fore. Also we acknowledge the efforts of the *Star*'s scanner Paul Wilson, its picture desk man Tony Adams and Fran Cartwright from the library department.

We're sure neither they nor Albion supporters will be disappointed with this end product.

Introduction

IT WAS probably at the official launch of *Albion Memories* in 1998 that the commitment to produce this second book was made. In fact, it was only a few days later that Albion were asking us at the *Express & Star* when a volume two might be hitting the shelves.

No wonder. Anyone present at that signing session attended by so many stars of yesteryear were reminded of the depth of interest in the club and the affection they command. It was a bumper turn-out.

Hundreds of fans queued on a cold November day for their copy of the book and the chance to have it autographed by an extremely patient array of players who would have cost millions and millions between them on today's transfer market. Yes, the huge fan presence caused us and the club some problems that afternoon and early evening! And, when a second launch was arranged for those disappointed the first time, the crowds were huge once again.

Albion Memories was a big success and a decision was very quickly taken to work on a follow-up. The extensive *Express & Star* picture library was to be 'raided' once again.

With a volume two, though, came some difficulties. We had used around 450 photographs in that well-received publication and it was going to take a major effort to turn up several hundred more for supporters to pore over.

Thankfully, with the help of Albion supporters and our friends in the rest of the newspaper industry, we believe we have put together an even more exclusive collection of pictures, the vast majority of which have probably not been seen by fans.

It has taken the best part of three years to compile this publication – a period in which Albion, thankfully, have shown signs of recovery – but we at the *Express & Star* are immensely proud to have our name attached to what we believe is a fitting tribute to Hawthorns glories down the generations.

We trust supporters will enjoy this journey through the club's distinguished history, complete with its cup triumphs, its European adventures and its challenges for the League Championship.

And, at the end of it, we hope they will be asking us about a volume three…

Glorious Beginnings

Albion were among the prizes in 1888 as they won the FA Cup for the first time, beating the Preston Invincibles after losing in the previous two Finals. They also lifted the more modest West Bromwich Charity Cup and were invited to contest the grandly-named Championship of the World against none other than Scottish club Renton at Hampden Park! Albion, who lost 4-1, are represented in this 1888 picture by (back row from left): Woodhall, Timmins, Perry, Aldridge, H. Green, Horton, Paddock. Front: T. Green, Bayliss, Roberts, Pearson.

An 1892 photograph comprising (back row from left): R. J. Hughes (committee), J. Lavender (committee), M. D. Nicholson, J. Reader, Councillor Phillips (committee), J. E. Stalton (committee), W. Paddock (trainer). Middle: W. Bassett, R. McLeod, W. Groves, T. Pearson, J. Geddes, C. Perry (captain). Front: T. McCulloch, J. Reynolds, F. Dyer.

From the mid-1890s are (from left): Perry, Simmons, Jones, Reader, Bassett, Flewitt, McKenzie, Richards, Garfield, Cave, Dunn. Albion won the FA Cup in 1888 and 1892, the Finals taking place at Kennington Oval against Preston and Aston Villa respectively.

In the Wembley Habit

The foundations of an unhappy relegation season. Albion, in striped shirts, battle it out in a 1-1 draw at Cardiff on 4 September 1926. A goal by Jack Byers brought the Baggies their reward but they went down to the Second Division the following spring with a total of only 30 points. The Albion man (right) is skipper and centre-half Fred Reed, who later became the club's trainer.

Another trip to South Wales, this one a defeat. Swansea Town provide the opposition on 3 March 1928, in a Division Two game that went the home side's way, 3-2, Jimmy Cookson netting both Albion goals. The Mancunian scored 92 times in only 103 League appearances for the club and, having previously played for Chesterfield, reached the fastest century of League goals in history.

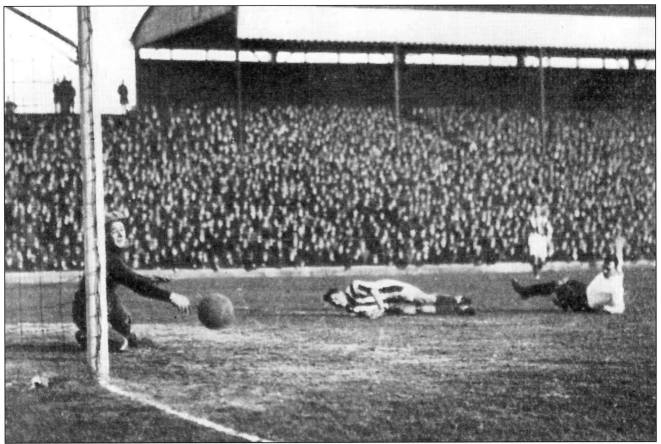

A near thing in Albion's 4-0 home victory over Fulham on 10 March 1928. The Baggies were in their first season back in the Second Division at the time and had a fixture list containing Clapton Orient, South Shields and Swansea Town. They finished eighth and didn't face the Londoners again in the League for 11 seasons. Jimmy Cookson is the Albion player. *Picture courtesy of Ken Coton.*

A close escape for Blues in the 1931 FA Cup Final, as a stooping Joe Carter, backed up by W. G. Richardson, fails to add his name to the score-sheet. Aston-born Carter, an inside-right who made 451 senior appearances for the Baggies, won three England caps in the late 1920s and also played for the Football League. Richardson scored both goals in this Final as Birmingham were defeated 2-1.

Nice to see you so far from home! Albion skipper Tommy Glidden, who played 479 competitive appearances for the Baggies and later became a director, marks the club's first appearance at Wembley meeting his Birmingham counterpart Ned Barkas before the 1931 FA Cup Final. Blues were probably favourites as they were a top-flight club and their opponents were then in the Second Division. The referee is Mr A. Kingscott of Derby.

More headaches for Blues keeper Harry Hibbs as he collects under pressure from Stan Wood, the man nicknamed 'The Singing Winger'. The tricky outside-left piled up 280 League and Cup matches for the club and, like Carter, Glidden and W. G. Richardson, also played a week later when Albion made history by becoming the first side to win promotion from the Second Division in the same season as lifting the FA Cup.

Birmingham players are heavily outnumbered as the leaping Joe Carter heads clear a corner watched by team-mates (from left) Bert Trentham, Billy Richardson and George Shaw. Richardson, from Great Bridge in the Black Country, was no relation to W. G. but a much younger brother of Sammy Richardson, the family duo totalling more than 560 appearances for the club. The Blues player is Joe Bradford.

Geordie Tommy Glidden, Albion's greatest goal-scoring winger, clutches the FA Cup on the lap of honour that followed the Wembley victory over Blues. Glidden, the club's skipper in the 1931 and 1935 finals, died in 1974, having received a special award two years earlier when he celebrated 50 years' loyal service at The Hawthorns.

Chelsea's defence come under pressure from the great W. G. Richardson during an Albion attack in their 3-2 defeat in the capital on 31 March 1934. Richardson netted one of Albion's goals and was a frequent scorer at Stamford Bridge. He marked his debut with a brace in a 6-1 Boxing Day home win over Millwall in 1929.

With Wembley in the air once again after Albion had beaten Port Vale 2-1, Sheffield United 7-1, Stockport 5-0, Preston 1-0 and Bolton 2-0 to reach the 1935 FA Cup Final against Sheffield Wednesday, it was time for different modes of relaxation for their players. Above, Yorkshireman George Shaw, a full-back who had helped Huddersfield to three successive League titles in the 1920s and who was to play more than 400 games for Albion and one for England, was happy to be pictured with wife and baby at home.

Shaw's fellow full-back Bert Trentham, who played in 272 League and FA Cup games for the club and represented the Football League, took Albion's international goalkeeper Harold Pearson for a drive. Tamworth-born Pearson, who made 303 senior appearances for the club, was the son of veteran Hawthorns keeper Hubert Pearson (377 Baggies games) and cousin of Birmingham and England keeper Harry Hibbs, opposing him in the 1931 FA Cup Final.

It's ukulele time for Albion centre-half Bill Richardson, surrounded by his mother, father, wife, brother and sister. Richardson, played in 352 first-team games and was part of the squad who made history by winning the FA Cup and promotion in 1931.

Another type of cup is on the minds of (from left) Tipton-born left-half Jim 'Iron' Edwards, Handsworth-born inside-left Ted Sandford and right-half Jimmy 'Spud' Murphy. Edwards and Murphy played well over 200 games for the club and England international Sandford more than 300. Murphy also played 15 times for Wales, managing them to the 1958 World Cup finals and serving as No 2 to Matt Busby at Manchester United around the time of the Munich air disaster.

White-shirted Sheffield Wednesday players are powerless to prevent Teddy Sandford's goal that made it 1-1 in the 1935 FA Cup Final at Wembley – an equaliser Albion supporters eagerly acclaimed. But they were silenced as Wednesday recovered their composure to win 4-2, Sheffield-born Wally Boyes scoring the Throstles' second in a game that thrilled the 93,204 crowd.

Albion's players and administrative staff line up for an annual photograph in the late 1930s. The club had followed their 1930-31 promotion and FA Cup double with successive First Division finishes of sixth, fourth, seventh and ninth before the going became much tougher. They were 18th in 1935-36, then 16th the following year before finishing 22nd and bottom in 1937-38. With the war intervening, they didn't regain their top-flight place until 1949.

Post-War Consolidation

Billy Elliott gets the cold water treatment from W. G. Richardson in The Hawthorns bath in the late 1940s. The two men had two things in common – they were both from the north of England and both might well have achieved more international recognition. Centre-forward Richardson won only one full cap while outside-right Elliott, whose haul of 157 goals from 330 games included a brilliant wartime record, represented his country only while the hostilities were on.

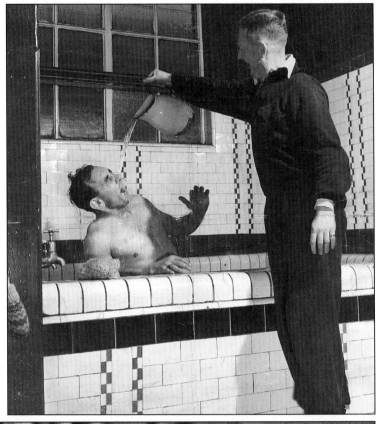

Anxious looks from the sidelines as Albion and Cardiff City battle it out in a Hawthorns replay in their FA Cup third-round clash in January 1950. The newly-promoted Throstles had emerged with a 2-2 draw in South Wales but slipped 1-0 at the second attempt – a pattern that was to be followed precisely against Derby County the year after. Closest to the camera, in the days when there was only one bench, are Albion trainer Fred Reed and his Cardiff counterpart Walter Robbins, who played for Albion in the 1930s. W. G. Richardson is behind in the trilby.

Albion secretary Eph Smith (right) and the man who was to succeed him in the post in 1960, his brother-in-law Alan Everiss, monitor The Hawthorns' new turnstile accumulator machine in 1949. The Everiss story is a truly remarkable one, the family maintaining a strong link with the club for more than 100 years – Alan from an office-boy in 1933 to the status of life member from 1980 to his death in the late 1990s and his father Fred from 1896 in a Hawthorns career spanning more than 50 years and including a lengthy stint as secretary-manager.

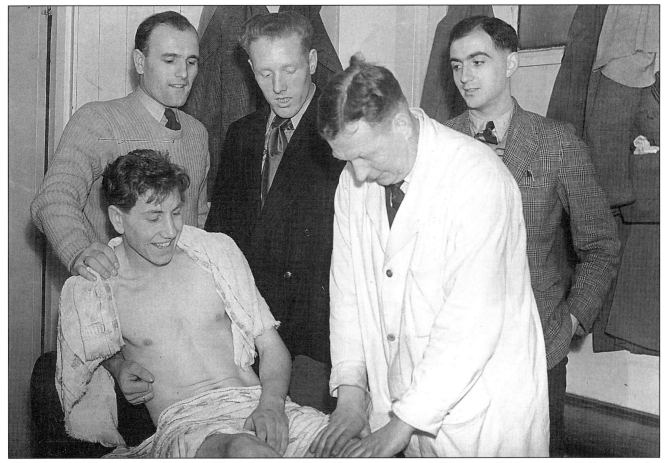

Billy 'Ginger' Richardson was not only a brilliant player for Albion. The man who scored 228 goals in 354 League and FA Cup games for the club between 1929 and 1939 also had healing hands! 'W. G.' served the Baggies for another decade and a half after the war, chiefly as trainer-coach – the role in which he is pictured working on Johnny Nicholls in this early 1950s shot. In the background are Norman Heath, Les Horne and Geoff Richards.

This time it's the feet that are being worked on by W. G. Richardson, the Albion great who died while playing in a 1959 charity match at a time when he was still on the club's pay-roll. Feeling the benefit here in 1950-51 is Frank Griffin, the outside-right who scored the club's 1954 Cup Final winner and who was to amass 52 goals in 275 appearances for them.

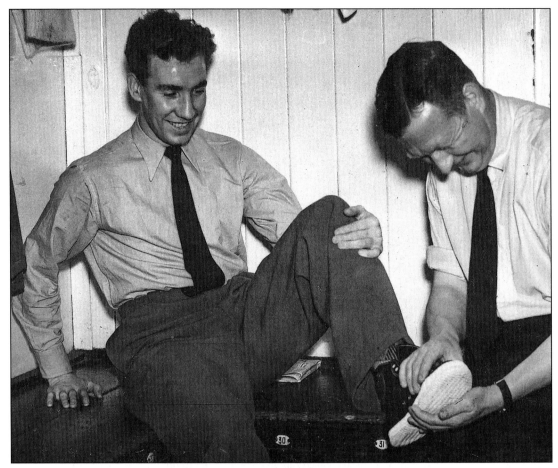

George Lee had good reason to remember this First Division visit to Liverpool on 18 February 1950. It was the day the left-winger, challenged here by centre-half Lawrie Hughes, scored the first of his 59 League goals for the club. The game came during a miserable run of 11 successive matches without a win, this one ending in a 2-1 defeat.

A Hawthorns pep-talk in a 1950-51 season in which Albion were destined to finish a mediocre 16th in the First Division. From left with W. G. Richardson (trainer) are Gerry Summers, Wilf Carter, Tim Rawlings, Vic Willies, Ken Hodgkisson, Reg Davies and Allan Crowshaw – a group of players who made little more than 130 appearances for the club between them.

Stan Rickaby, whose 205 senior Albion games included a run of 143 successive First Division outings up to November 1953, boots clear under pressure from Arsenal's Jimmy Logie in a 3-0 First Division defeat at Highbury on 30 September 1950. The Teesside-born right-back, who played once for England and emigrated to Australia in 1969, was unlucky to miss the 1954 FA Cup Final through injury.

White Hart Lane woe for Albion on 17 March 1951, as they are sunk in the mud in a 5-0 thrashing by a Tottenham side en route for the First Division championship in their first season up. Jack Vernon, the Belfast-born centre-half who won 22 full international caps and skippered Albion to promotion in 1948-49, fails to prevent Len Duquemin from completing his hat-trick.

A safe catch by Albion goalkeeper Norman Heath, under the watchful eye of Jack Vernon, as Fulham press in the League game at Craven Cottage in late September 1951. The Baggies, then managed by Jack Smith, had won by the odd goal at the venue for the previous five seasons but went down 1-0 to a team who ended the season relegated. Bedford Jezzard is the Fulham player.

No way through! Villa's defenders are back in force to shut out Ronnie Allen as Albion seek a way to goal in their 2-1 derby defeat at The Hawthorns on 1 December 1951. It's a similar story as Stan Lynn (No 2 in the picture above) prepares to take the ball out of danger (below) despite the presence of George Lee. The Baggies' goal came from Allen.

Fashion accessories for supporters 1952 style. Thick woollen scarves and rattles were very much the vogue around the time of Albion's FA Cup fourth-round journey to St James's Park almost half a century ago. But it's not Newcastle that these ladies were waiting to see their heroes playing against. The Geordies' smaller brethren and temporary ground-sharers Gateshead were the opposition as the Baggies progressed to a 2-0 victory thanks to two Ronnie Allen goals in front of a 38,681 crowd.

With Ray Barlow looking on, Ronnie Allen and Reg 'Paddy' Ryan are put through their paces by trainer W. G. Richardson before Albion's 1952-53 FA Cup fourth-round marathon against Chelsea. Also partially in view is Johnny Nicholls. In an amazing saga of a tie, the sides drew at Stamford Bridge, The Hawthorns and Villa Park before Chelsea won 4-0 in a third replay at Highbury.

Wembley Revisited

Where stage and sport meet. Vic Buckingham (right), Albion manager from 1953 to 1959, is locked in conversation with fellow Londoner Tommy Steele, who played in a showbiz football team and got to know members of The Hawthorns camp. Buckingham, who died in 1994, had a varied managerial career that also took him to Barcelona, Seville, Greece and Ajax.

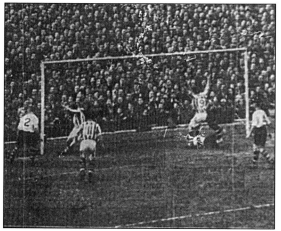

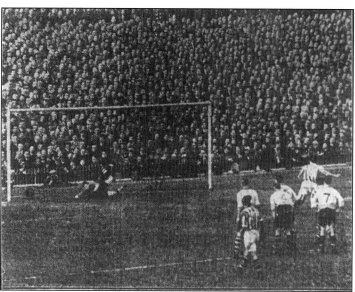

A close-run thing! Albion, having beaten Charlton, Rotherham, Newcastle and Tottenham to go into the last four of the 1953-54 FA Cup, were expected to overpower Third Division North outfit Port Vale with something to spare in the semi-final. The 27 March tie, in front of 68,221 at Villa Park, was anything but straightforward, though, with Albert Leake giving the underdogs a first-half lead they held until Jimmy Dudley's lob – one of only 11 goals the Glaswegian wing-half scored in 320 Albion appearances – drops into the net (left). The winner came from the penalty spot from Ronnie Allen (right), who was born in the Potteries town of Fenton and played early in his career for Vale. *Pictures courtesy of the Evening Sentinel.*

Straight down the middle. Reg 'Paddy' Ryan brings admiring glances from his colleagues as he drives off at Reading's Sonning Golf Club two days before the 1954 FA Cup Final victory over Preston. Albion were in Berkshire as part of their preparations for Wembley, where Dubliner Ryan – winner of 17 international caps – played at inside-right. Also in view are (from left) Stuart Williams, Frank Griffin, Len Millard, Wilf Carter, trainer Arthur Fitton and George Lee.

Getting set for departure amid the usual formalities... skipper Len Millard adds his autograph to a signed football, watched by (from left) Jimmy Dugdale, Frank Griffin, George Lee, Jimmy Dudley, Stuart Williams, Paddy Ryan, Ray Barlow, Jim Sanders, Johnny Nicholls, Ronnie Allen, Joe Kennedy and trainer Arthur Fitton.

On to Wembley for a look at the hallowed turf. Goalkeeper Jim Sanders tests the surface, watched by (from left) Frank Griffin, Stan Rickaby, Jimmy Dugdale, Ray Barlow, Albion director Horace Thursfield, Jimmy Dudley and Johnny Nicholls.

Striding across the lush acres… "feels great!" From left: Len Millard, Jimmy Dudley, Frank Griffin and Johnny Nicholls.

Hope we're not walking down these famous 39 steps empty-handed! Albion players and officials take a pre-match look at the Royal Box floral arrangements.

Back to the hotel for rest and recreation in front of a relatively new luxury item – a TV set!

Another pre-match shot of Albion's relaxing players, this time on Cup Final eve. Pictured ready for dinner are (from left) Johnny Nicholls, Jimmy Dudley, Ronnie Allen, Frank Griffin, George Lee, Joe Kennedy, captain Len Millard and, in customary bow tie, goalkeeper Jim Sanders. All eight played in the 3-2 win over Preston.

Up for the Cup! Albion fans, including June Carter and Winnie Jeffries, chat to the driver of their steam train after disembarking at Euston on their way to the big Wembley clash with Preston.

Another batch of Albion fans arrive in the capital, excited and confident about the ninth of the Baggies' ten FA Cup Final appearances to date.

Jim Sanders takes off but can't stop the Angus Morrison header that made it 1-1 only a minute after Ronnie Allen had scored his first goal midway through the first half. Ray Barlow, Joe Kennedy and Frank Griffin are the three helpless Albion outfield players.

Left-winger George Lee, supported by Johnny Nicholls, crosses for Ronnie Allen to open the Wembley scoring with the first of his two goals. The centre-forward's second was a famously photographed penalty that made it 2-2.

The magical moment… the Queen Mother, alongside Sir Stanley Rous, presents winning Albion skipper Len Millard with the spoils of success. Second in line is Jimmy Dudley, a wing-half who was halfway through an unbroken run of 166 consecutive League appearances (then a club record) at the time of the Final.

Celebration time for Albion right-winger Frank Griffin (with cigarette) and left-back Len Millard, with wives Mary (right) and Ruth respectively. Griffin hit the winner at Wembley – undoubtedly the highlight of his Throstles career of 275 senior appearances and 52 goals.

Victory speech… Major H. Wilson Keys, Albion's chairman from 1947 to 1963, praises the team at the traditional Cup Final night dinner for their feat in putting the silverware in West Bromwich hands for the fourth time – and the first time in 23 years.

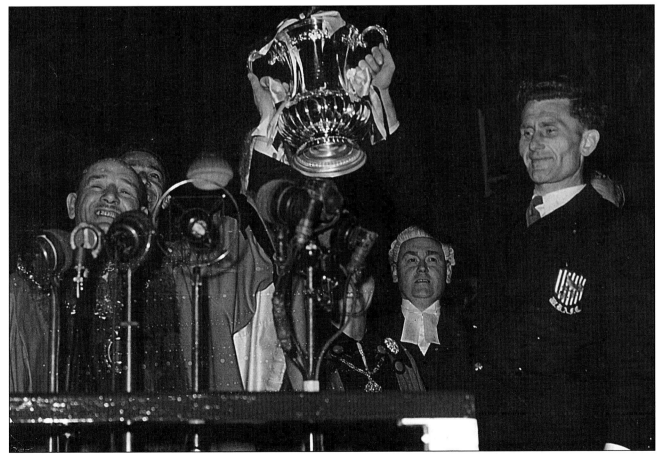

Glad we could bring something home to share with you! Proud Albion captain and left-back Len Millard, who made 477 appearances for the club in the League, FA Cup and Charity Shield, shows off the Cup, with the help of West Bromwich's Mayor.

One for the supporters as the Cup is paraded by open-top bus round the streets of West Bromwich. Getting a touch of the big prize are Ronnie Allen, Len Millard, Jim Sanders (in trademark bow tie) and Frank Griffin.

A Major Force

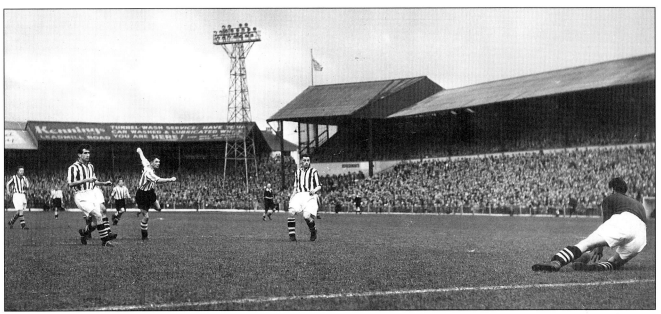

A moment of danger to Albion's goal during their 2-1 win at Sheffield United on 4 September 1954 – from a man who was to become a well-known Hawthorns figure. Blades legend Jimmy Hagan, who also collected one England cap before embarking on a managerial career that included four years at Albion, sees a shot well saved by Jim Sanders. Albion's season had started with defeats at Sunderland and Newcastle but the club still recorded seven wins before the end of September. *Picture courtesy of Sheffield Star.*

A determined stretch by Paddy Ryan as he attempts a shot at Chelsea's goal, despite the presence of full-back Stan Willemse, during the 3-3 First Division draw on 2 October 1954. Albion's first visit to London since FA Cup Final glory put Ronnie Allen, George Lee and Len Millard on the score-sheet and took the club's League goal tally – boosted by a 6-4 win over Leicester the weekend before – to 27 in nine games.

Derby joy for Albion, albeit briefly, as George Lee rifles in their second goal in The Hawthorns First Division clash with Aston Villa on 30 October 1954. Paddy Ryan is also pictured as keeper Ken Jones's dive and defender Stan Lynn's sliding intervention come to nothing. Ronnie Allen scored the FA Cup holders' other goal in what was their fourth successive defeat.

Paddy Ryan challenges for a high ball during an Albion game at Cardiff in the early 1950s. Looking on from the right of the picture are a leaping Jack Vernon and a static Ray Barlow, the stylish Swindon-born wing-half who won only one full England cap in a career that brought him 482 senior appearances for the club (48 goals) as well as, in the late 1950s, The Hawthorns captaincy. *Picture courtesy of Western Mail & Echo Limited.*

The second half of a West Midlands derby double-header. Albion, their grip on the FA Cup broken by visiting Charlton in the fourth round, beat visiting Wolves with a single George Lee goal on 16 March 1955, but went down 3-0 here at Aston Villa three days later. Jim Sanders moves in the right direction but is well beaten by Stan Lynn's penalty. After promotion in 1949, the Baggies had a dire League record at Villa, losing six and drawing two of eight trips.

Skirmish in the snow as Ray Barlow (left) tangles with full-back Jeff Hall – an England international right-back who was to die of polio – in Albion's 1-0 FA Cup fifth-round defeat against Birmingham at The Hawthorns on 18 February 1956. The Baggies, watched here by a 57,213 gate, had beaten another West Midlands club, Wolves, and Portsmouth in the earlier rounds. In those days, the home team changed colours in the Cup in the event of a colour clash.

Left-winger George Lee skips round Arsenal right-back Stan Charlton during Albion's 4-1 defeat at Highbury on 1 September 1956. Lee, who played almost 300 games for the club, was to lose his place to Roy Horobin over the coming months but returned to The Hawthorns for a spell as trainer-coach at the end of the decade.

Goal coming up for Ronnie Allen as he evades the body of goalkeeper Jack Kelsey to score Albion's first in their 2-2 FA Cup quarter-final draw at home to Arsenal in March 1957. More than 53,000 were present and 58,757 turned up for the Highbury replay, in which Albion won against a side who had already done a League double over them that season. In the background is Brian Whitehouse.

Another scene from the Gunners' FA Cup visit to the Black Country as Ray Barlow and his goalkeeper Jim Sanders combine to deny Derek Tapscott and leave the Arsenal forward in some discomfort. Albion were in good goal-scoring form at the time, putting four past Chelsea, Luton and Sunderland just before or just after this tie.

FA Cup derbies became very much part of Albion life in the second half of the 1950s, the Baggies making it to the semi-final in 1956-57 and a clash with Aston Villa at neutral Molineux. Brian Whitehouse, later to serve Villa as a scout, scored both Albion goals in a 2-2 draw while, at the other end, Johnny Dixon saw this header blocked by Don Howe, watched by Ray Barlow, No 11 Peter McParland and Albion centre-half Joe Kennedy. Irishman McParland scored two equalisers for a largely outplayed Villa side, the second with only five minutes left.

Joe Kennedy heads clear in a tense St Andrew's semi-final replay on the Thursday afternoon of 28 March 1957, as Ray Barlow and Villa's Johnny Dixon look on. The match was Albion's ninth in that season's competition, the side also having needed replays against Doncaster, Blackpool and Arsenal.

The goal that broke Albion hearts and sent Villa to Wembley, where they beat Manchester United 2-1 in their first Final appearance since 1924. Billy Myerscough is on his knees but his 38th minute header has already dissected the despairing Jim Sanders and Len Millard for the game's deciding moment.

Pushing for a way back into the tie. Brian Whitehouse and right-back Don Howe add to the pressure on Villa goalkeeper Nigel Sims in front of 58,067 enthralled fans at St Andrew's. Albion, although unchanged from the first match five days earlier, were hampered by an injury to Ronnie Allen that left the centre-forward a passenger for much of the game. Allen was concussed in a challenge with his former Hawthorns team-mate Jimmy Dugdale, who went on several weeks later to add another Cup winners' medal to the one gained with Albion in 1954.

Albion escape further damage in their barely deserved 1-0 defeat as Peter McParland lets fly with a clear shot that beats the outstretched leg of Don Howe and causes goalkeeper Jim Sanders plenty of concern. But, somehow, the ball stayed out. Vic Buckingham's side even finished one place below Villa in the middle of a First Division won for the second year running by Manchester United.

Not just for the cameras... dressing-room cricket became a pre-match ritual for Albion in 1957-58. Playing a straight bat here is Ronnie Allen, with (left to right) Roy Horobin, Stuart Williams, Derek Kevan, Frank Griffin, Jimmy Dudley, Bobby Robson and Maurice Setters waiting for an edge. The Baggies subsequently demolished Manchester City 5-1 in an FA Cup third-round clash – the third successive game in which they had scored five.

High emotion hangs in the air as Manchester United and Albion slug it out in an FA Cup sixth-round replay at Old Trafford on 5 March 1958. Only a month earlier, the Munich air crash had claimed the lives of eight United players, with Dudley-born Duncan Edwards subsequently dying from his injuries. Right: The customary pre-match handshake between the skippers, Ray Barlow of Albion and Bill Foulkes of United in succession to the deceased Roger Byrne.

Harry Gregg, a hero on the snowy Munich runway, saves from Brian Whitehouse as Bobby Robson (centre) and Derek Kevan close in. Albion lost 1-0 to a last-gasp Colin Webster goal but won 4-0 at the same venue in the League three days later, many of their players subsequently expressing their surprise at the hostility of the Old Trafford crowd at a time when United were attracting so much public sympathy.

Big danger is looming for Albion goalkeeper Clive Jackman as Scottish international Jackie Henderson flashes a header past him in Arsenal's thrilling 4-3 First Division win at Highbury on 4 October 1958. Derek Kevan scored all three of Albion's goals and was on target in the 1-1 draw between the sides at The Hawthorns in the following February.

Moment of embarrassment for Albion's Clive Jackman as his error gifts the old enemy a Villa Park derby goal on 11 October 1958. It proved to be the last of the goalkeeper's 21 Baggies appearances before, amid injury problems, he made way for Ray Potter. And at least it was a winning finish, Albion running out 4-1 victors against a side who had been a jinx on them in the Second City but whose 21-year First Division stay was about to end.

Sixties Rebuilding

It looks like one of The Hawthorns' more one-sided games as four Albion players find themselves distanced from their opponents in the Easter Tuesday League clash with Birmingham on 19 April 1960. Pictured are (from left) Dave Burnside, Derek Kevan, Derek Hogg and Bobby Robson in a game that ended 1-1, Kevan scoring for one of 29 times that season. The previous day, Kevan and Ronnie Allen had scored hat-tricks in a 7-1 romp at St Andrew's!

Unhappy scene for Gordon Clark's Albion at Stamford Bridge on 3 December 1960, as Jimmy Greaves scores one of the goals with which Chelsea ran out crushing 7-1 victors. Jock Wallace is the beaten goalkeeper and Bobby Robson the man chasing back in vain in Greaves's wake. It was a fourth successive defeat for the Throstles, who were destined to finish tenth in the table.

An historic moment as Ronnie Allen forces the ball past goalkeeper Sid Farrimond and covering defender Bill Eckersley in Albion's 3-2 First Division home victory over Bolton on 25 February 1961. It was the last of The Hawthorns legend's then-record 208 League goals for the club and came in his final Baggies appearance before joining Crystal Palace. All told, he scored 234 goals in 458 games for them, played five games for England and was the only man to score in each of the first 20 post-war seasons of English football. Allen died in the summer of 2001, aged 72.

A few minutes after Ronnie Allen had scored his last Albion goal, Bobby Hope notched his first for the club with this cross-shot out of nothing. The midfielder also scored in the win at West Ham the following Saturday, having made his debut at the age of 16 at home to Arsenal on the last day of the previous season. He was to play 403 senior games for Albion, his 42 goals including the club's first in European competition – away to Utrecht of Holland in 1966-67.

Vital block by Don Howe in the 1-1 First Division draw against Manchester United on 7 October 1961 – Gordon Clark's last match as Hawthorns boss. The United player thinking he's about to score is Albert Quixall while goalkeeper Tony Millington and full-back Stuart Williams look on. Wolverhampton-born Howe played 379 first-team matches for Albion from 1955 to 1964, many as captain, and returned in 1971 to manage the club. The other United man is Alex Dawson.

Goals continued to come thick and fast after Archie Macaulay had been appointed as new Albion boss, Derek Kevan scoring a hat-trick in this 3-1 home victory over Sheffield United on 18 November 1961. Here, Keith Smith, scorer of 30 goals in only 63 League appearances for the club, fires narrowly wide. Albion were to finish the season in ninth place and the Blades in fifth.

The combined attentions of Stuart Williams and a stooping Stan Jones fail to stop Barry Bridges beating goalkeeper Tony Millington for one of Chelsea's four goals in their emphatic First Division victory over the Throstles at Stamford Bridge on 25 November 1961. Chuck Drury and Bobby Tambling are in the background. Chelsea were still relegated that season.

Back in London, this time for a victory. Derek 'The Tank' Kevan, watched by Keith Smith, just fails to connect with this cross at Highbury on 3 February 1962. Arsenal duo Jack Kelsey and Dave Bacuzzi may have been relieved on this occasion but Albion still won 1-0 with a goal in his debut season by winger Clive Clark, who had also scored against the Gunners at The Hawthorns.

Strange coincidences as Albion crash 4-2 to Tottenham in the FA Cup fifth round on 17 February 1962. The Baggies had previously lost to 1960-61 Double winners Spurs by the same score in the League, on each occasion their goals coming from Derek Kevan and Keith Smith, who are seen here with Peter Baker, Danny Blanchflower and Maurice Norman. This gate of 54,992 has not been bettered at The Hawthorns since.

Revenge for Albion as they run out 2-1 winners at Spurs in April 1962, despite this close-quarters save by Bill Brown from Clive Clark. Two-goal Derek Kevan is pictured tangling in the background with Maurice Norman. Kevan topped Albion's scoring charts that season with 33 League goals, this result doing nothing for the title hopes of a Spurs side who were Double champions at the time but were to finish third behind Ipswich and Burnley while retaining the FA Cup.

Between their victory at Tottenham and this 2-0 home win over Fulham only three days later, Albion switched back to striped sleeves and squeezed in a 2-1 Easter Monday triumph at Fulham! Here, Alec Jackson shoots over England's 1966 World Cup Final No 2 George Cohen and over the bar. Both goals for an Albion side who ended the season with five straight wins and in ninth place, came from the also-pictured Kevan.

Chuck Drury tries to cut out a chipped pass from Denis Law during Albion's First Division clash at Manchester United on the opening day of the 1962-63 campaign. Law was making his United debut after being signed for £115,000 and scored one of the two goals by which Albion trailed in only six minutes. But strikes by Derek Kevan and Keith Smith took a point off a United side who had Johnny Giles on their right wing and who would win the FA Cup that season.

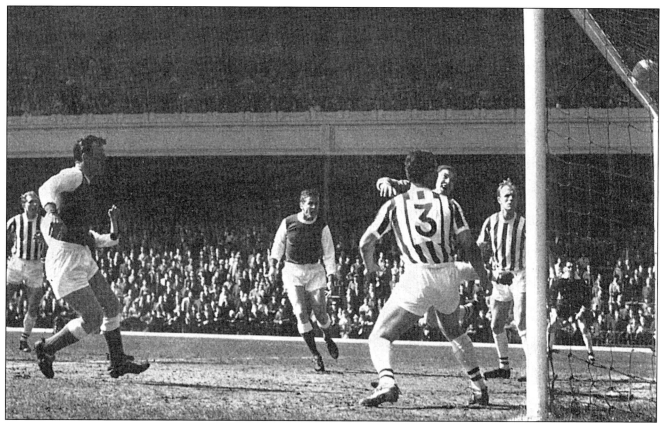

The reign starts in the sun! Jimmy Hagan, formerly boss at Peterborough, took over as Albion manager just before the club's Good Friday visit to Arsenal on 12 April 1963. And it was a tough start as the Gunners scored after only 40 seconds! Albion were destined to go down 3-2 and lose their first three games under Hagan, their Highbury eclipse helped by this Alan Skirton goal watched by Bobby Cram, Graham Williams, Ray Potter and Don Howe.

In front of the quaint Craven Cottage, Graham Williams holds off Pat O'Connell in Albion's 2-2 draw at Fulham in their final match of a mediocre 1962-63. Alec Jackson and Ronnie Fenton scored and Williams went on to lift the FA Cup five years to the day after this match. His last Cup outing for Albion came at Fulham the year after. *Picture courtesy of Ken Coton.*

The closest of close shaves as a Jimmy Melia shot skids inches past the post in Albion's October 1963 1-0 defeat away to a Liverpool side destined to win the championship. Graham Williams is the defender nearest the ball, with a partly-hidden Terry Simpson, Chuck Drury, Ray Potter, Doug Fraser and Stan Jones also pictured, along with Ian St John and Roger Hunt. This was Tony Brown's third League game for Albion. True to form, he had scored in the previous two! *Picture courtesy of Liverpool Post and Echo.*

A brave take by Ray Potter at the feet of Tottenham forward Bobby Smith in Albion's 2-0 League win at White Hart Lane on 28 December 1963 – Spurs' first defeat in 20 home games. Looking on are Don Howe, Doug Fraser and No 5 Stan Jones, the two teams having drawn 4-4 at The Hawthorns on Boxing Day. Kent-born Potter played 238 games for the Throstles and was a League ever-present for them from the middle of 1962-63 to October 1965.

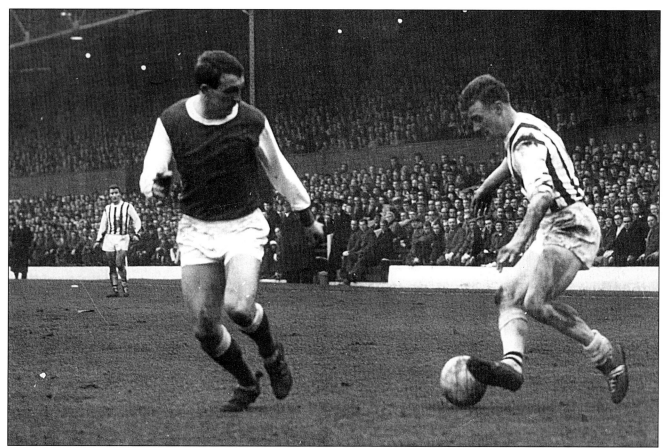

Clive Clark teases his marker in a thrilling 3-3 FA Cup fourth-round draw against Arsenal at The Hawthorns on 25 January 1964. Ronnie Fenton, John Kaye and Stan Jones (with one of only three goals in 267 first-team games) were on the mark for Albion, who twice hit back from two goals adrift, only to lose the replay 2-0. Albion's players had gone on strike several weeks earlier in protest at manager Jimmy Hagan's refusal to allow them to wear tracksuit bottoms in training.

Jimmy Greaves holds off Stan Jones and Bobby Cram in the White Hart Lane sunshine to beat the heroic Ray Potter for his 100th League goal for Tottenham. This 44th-minute strike was the only goal of a game played on 19 September 1964. Remarkably, this seventh First Division game of the season was fulfilled by precisely the same Baggies side who had figured in the previous six.

Not a great match for black and white TV! Ray Potter watches a Derek Temple header flash wide during Albion's 3-2 Boxing Day defeat at Everton in 1964. Jimmy Gabriel is the other Toffees player pictured while red-shirted Albion wing-halves Terry Simpson and Doug Fraser are there as cover. It was obviously the era for white Christmases because the game was later marked by a snow storm. *Picture courtesy of Liverpool Post and Echo.*

A first glimpse of the new all-white change strip that was to become regarded as lucky during Albion's 1968 FA Cup glories. The new look was chosen for this First Division clash at the Victoria Ground on 16 January 1965 – and it wasn't a promising start. Stoke won 2-0 despite this clean catch by Ray Potter from No 9 John Ritchie, watched by Doug Fraser, Peter Dobing, Terry Simpson and Harry Burrows. *Picture courtesy of Evening Sentinel.*

Goalkeeper Ray Potter makes a courageous dive near the boot of Burnley centre-forward Andy Lochhead in a 1-0 Albion League victory at Turf Moor on 6 February 1965. The only goal came from winger Ken Foggo while Terry Simpson keeps watch over this near miss. The wing-half also served Walsall and was making one of the last of his 77 senior appearances for the club.

Bobby Cram, Doug Fraser, a falling Ray Potter and Terry Simpson are powerless to prevent John Robson scoring the first goal in Albion's 3-0 beating at Blackpool in March 1965. The Seasiders' No 8 is Alan Ball, who tormented a Baggies side languishing in a run of seven defeats in eight First Division away games. Ball, an England World Cup hero in 1966, was to score four times for Everton at The Hawthorns in one League game – won 6-2 by the visitors – in 1968.

Painful point of contact for Gerry Howshall as he halts West Ham's John Sissons in a Good Friday morning clash at Upton Park in April 1965. The flailing left boot wasn't the only uncomfortable part of the day for the flame-haired right-half, who made 43 League appearances for Albion. West Ham, 1964 FA Cup winners and 1965 European Cup Winners' Cup champions, won 6-1, Brian Dear scoring five times in 21 minutes from just before half-time.

The day after their West Ham walloping, Albion took a good point from a 2-2 draw with title-chasing Chelsea at Stamford Bridge. George Graham is the player climbing highest in this melee that also involves Stan Jones (nearest camera) and Ray Potter. Albion, wearing white shorts, are also represented in the picture by goalscorer Gerry Howshall and Bobby Cram.

Lion-hearted Albion forward John Kaye, later converted by Alan Ashman to a defensive wing-half, is addressed by Alf Ramsey at Roehampton during the build-up to England's Wembley friendly against Austria in October 1965. Kaye lost out to Chelsea's Barry Bridges, though, remained uncapped and had to be content with two outings in the Football League side, although he had been a member of Ramsey's original World Cup 40 in 1966.

My ball! Rick Sheppard, playing only the fourth of his 54 Albion games, hangs on in a 2-1 away defeat against Tottenham on 30 October 1965. Rival centre-halves Stan Jones and Laurie Brown are the players in closest attendance while, to the right, is Albion scorer Ray Crawford. Spurs' win took their magnificent unbeaten home run to 33 games. Sheppard died of a heart attack late in 1998.

Ray Wilson and Graham Lovett both scored their first senior goals – Wilson's coming in only his second first-team game – when Albion subjected Fulham to fireworks on 6 November 1965. The home side ran out handsome 6-2 winners against a team containing their former wing-half Bobby Robson, who scored right at the end. In this first-half scare, Rick Sheppard, Stan Jones and Bobby Cram usher a centre to safety as John Dempsey hovers. *Picture courtesy of Ken Coton.*

Nervous moments for Albion as they come under pressure from Ray Charnley and the grounded John Robson in their 1-1 draw at Blackpool on 13 November 1965. Stan Jones tries to cover while Rick Sheppard makes his move, with Graham Lovett right behind him. Tony Brown scored Albion's goal as their season continued to level out after they had led the table in early September.

Not what it seems! Tongue out as usual, Tony Brown looks on in anticipation as the ball rolls towards the net against Peterborough in the home leg of the 1965-66 League Cup semi-final. Brown did score – but with a header at the Birmingham Road End, not this effort – on a night when Jeff Astle completed a 2-1 victory. Albion, fired by Brown's hat-trick, won the second leg 4-2, 'Bomber' scoring in every round of the competition.

Another 1-1 draw in 1965-66, this time at frozen Old Trafford, Ray Fairfax, No 5 Stan Jones, Bobby Cram and No 4 Graham Lovett expressing their relief as a Manchester United effort from England winger John Connelly (left) flies over the bar at the Stretford End. Ray Crawford netted for Albion, as he did when they romped home 5-1 at Sunderland five days later.

A week after drawing at Liverpool, Albion suffered another early FA Cup exit when they crashed 3-0 at Second Division Bolton in the third round on 22 January 1966. Burnden Park had been carpeted in snow before the tie, which included a brace by Francis Lee, one goal by Brian Bromley and a lot of celebrations among the home fans. *Picture courtesy of Bolton Evening News*.

Ray Potter scoops the ball off David Ford's toe in the 2-1 First Division win at Sheffield Wednesday on 19 February 1966, as Graham Williams looks on. Hillsborough, a World Cup venue a few months later, became an unhappy ground for Albion, especially in the late 1960s, when they twice suffered late FA Cup exits. They didn't win there again until 2000-01. *Picture courtesy of Sheffield Star.*

Defenders Ray Fairfax (left) and Graham Williams find themselves under pressure from ex-England striker Johnny Byrne in the away first leg of Albion's League Cup Final against West Ham on 9 March 1966. It was one of Fairfax's 92 first-team appearances for a club who were beaten 2-1 by a last-gasp goal at Upton Park – Jeff Astle scoring for the visitors – before brilliantly burying the Hammers 4-1 in the second leg to put the first major silverware in The Hawthorns cabinet for 12 years. It was the first time Albion had entered the League Cup.

The great Gordon Banks, an England hero a few weeks later, is left floundering as John Kaye stabs in one of his two goals in Albion's 5-1 victory over Leicester on 22 April 1966. Graham Cross (left) and Peter Rodrigues are the equally helpless defenders. Jimmy Hagan's League Cup winners finished sixth in the table, their tally of 58 home League goals emerging as easily the highest in the top flight.

When Albion Had the Mersey 'Beat'!

It may have become difficult to believe in subsequent decades, but Albion were the scourge of Merseyside in the mid-1960s.

At home or away, they were feared opponents to both Liverpool and Everton, although the two Stanley Park neighbours were busy at the time accumulating trophies at a very healthy rate.

The Red half of the city celebrated First Division glory in both 1963-64 and 1965-66, on the first occasion in only their club's second season in the top flight after eight years in Division Two. Under the unique management of Bill Shankly, Liverpool also won the FA Cup in 1965 and were beaten finalists in the 1965-66 European Cup Winners' Cup.

Everton were determined not to be left in the role of bridesmaids and helped themselves to the First Division title both in 1962-63 – assisted by a late-season 4-0 win at The Hawthorns – and 1969-70, and to the FA Cup via a thrilling comeback against Sheffield Wednesday in 1966.

Albion, however, were no respecters of reputations in those entertaining years either side of England's World Cup triumph. In 20 meetings with Liverpool during that decade, they won seven, drew eight and lost only five.

In the mid-1960s, they recorded a hat-trick of 3-0 League victories over Shankly's formidable machine and famously had the Kop chanting 'West Brom, West Brom' after the one-sided win by that margin at Anfield near the end of 1964-65.

While Albion came out considerably better than even in their clashes with Liverpool, they were slightly behind against Everton, although good enough to send the Toffees home point-less from The Hawthorns on no fewer than six times out of ten and bold enough to feature in games of 3-2 (twice), 5-4 and 4-2 at Goodison Park.

And, of course, there was the ultimate satisfaction for Albion in 1967-68. Although, ironically, both Mersey clubs performed a League double over Alan Ashman's side that season, they had to admit second best to them in the FA Cup.

Liverpool, boasting the likes of Yeats, Smith, Callaghan, Milne, Thompson, Hunt and St John, were despatched to the Black Country for a sixth-round tie that ebbed and flowed, only for rival keepers John Osborne and Tommy Lawrence to cling bravely to clean sheets. In a Monday night replay in which Albion were given little chance of survival, Jeff Astle's header – and a goalless period of extra-time – brought about a 1-1 draw after Tony Hateley's opener in front of the Kop had apparently seen to it that the tie was going to form.

Then it was off ten nights later for a second replay at Maine Road that some Albion fans regard as the most gripping FA Cup tie the club have played in their lifetime.

Albion, again in their lucky all-white change strip, scored early through Astle, had their defence pierced once more by Hateley at the height of enormous Liverpool pressure before half-time but snatched a brilliantly executed winner through Clive Clark mid-way through the second half.

At that point, having come through three pulsating ties watched by a total of 155,000 fans, Ashman's men were beginning to dream that their name was already engraved on the Cup.

With one Mersey club accounted for and Birmingham's luckless semi-final challenge withstood, it was on to Wembley to try to deal with the other. Everton had won 6-2 against Albion in the League only a few weeks earlier, Alan Ball dancing across The Hawthorns to great effect as he netted a remarkable four-goal haul. But they found it much tougher going at the twin towers.

Even Albion supporters would admit the Final itself was not a classic but Astle's decider early in extra-time certainly did fit into that category – and their side had delivered against the odds once more, this time amid the highest stakes of all.

With the city of Liverpool at the forefront of pop music's 1960s explosion, Albion had become very adept at showing they had the Mersey 'beat'!

The *Express & Star* are grateful to their counterparts on the *Liverpool Daily Post and Echo*, who have provided the vast bulk of the photographs in this section.

Tony Millington guesses right, dives left and saves Jimmy Melia's penalty in Albion's home First Division win against Liverpool on 27 October 1962. The game's only goal came from Derek Kevan. Liverpool, under the legendary Bill Shankly, had only just arrived back in the top flight and were to be crowned champions 18 months later. Millington played only 40 games for Albion in addition to 21 for Wales.

Don Howe slides the ball away from Ian St John and away from danger as Liverpool press in a 2-2 midweek draw at Anfield on 20 March 1963. Albion, beaten 7-0 at Wolves in another League clash four days earlier, are also represented in the picture by Ron Bradley, Bobby Hope and No 4 Bobby Cram. The Baggies' goals came from Ronnie Fenton and Keith Smith.

It looks ominous for Albion as Ian St John hooks the ball goalwards, with Ray Potter out of position, in The Hawthorns meeting on 24 October 1964. But the effort was off-target and Jimmy Hagan's side won 3-0 with goals by Clive Clark (2) and Jeff Astle. Also in the photograph are (from left) Bobby Cram, Gerry Howshall, who had scored the winner at Villa the week before, Geoff Carter (background) and Geoff Strong.

Albion were the masters of Anfield on 7 April 1965. This appeal for a penalty by John Kaye, Jeff Astle and Ken Foggo came to nothing, but the Baggies still romped home 3-0 – and completed a tremendous double against Liverpool – thanks to goals by Kaye, Bobby Hope and Clive Clark. It was Liverpool's first home defeat for six months as they made good progress in the European Cup after winning the League the year before. A few weeks after this game, Bill Shankly's men lifted the FA Cup, having won 2-1 at The Hawthorns in round three.

Nervous moments in Everton's defence during Albion's 3-2 midweek win at Goodison Park on 7 September 1965. John Kaye, a scorer along with Tony Brown and Jeff Astle, is the man doing the harrying as Gordon West finds himself in a flap with his No 3 Ray Wilson – England's World Cup winning left-back – and fellow defender Brian Harris. Ken Foggo is the other Albion player pictured.

Albion had tasted 1965-66 life at the top of the First Division when they faced Everton in their return fixture on Wednesday, 15 September. They had gone into pole position by winning 4-3 at newly-promoted Northampton the previous Friday but had to settle for a 1-1 draw in their clash with the Merseysiders. Jeff Astle scored their goal, although not from this tussle with Brian Labone, watched by Graham Lovett.

Albion 3 Liverpool 0 – again! The Merseysiders' status as 1964 League champions and 1965 FA Cup winners counted for little at The Hawthorns on 23 October 1965 in the face of goals by Tony Brown, John Kaye and Clive Clark. What made the victory more worthy was that Liverpool were to win the title in this season as well. Here, Rick Sheppard looks unsure under pressure from Chris Lawler as Doug Fraser, Kaye, Ron Yeats, Stan Jones, a distant Clark and Geoff Strong look on.

The signs of mid-winter are clearly visible as Liverpool and Albion slug it out at freezing Anfield on 15 January 1966. Tony Brown, tracked from a distance by Ron Yeats, Gordon Milne and a hidden Tommy Smith, warms Throstles fans by driving his side into a 1-0 lead that they doubled through John Kaye by the quarter-hour mark.

More action from the same game as Bill Shankly's men turned up the heat themselves to salvage a 2-2 draw and cause some anxious moments like this one for Ray Potter. The goalkeeper eventually gathers as Milne, Ian St John and Roger Hunt wait for a slip while Bobby Hope, goalscorer John Kaye and Graham Lovett form the back-up cast.

22 April 1967 has emerged as a red-letter day for Albion – it was the last time they won at Anfield. Jeff Astle, seen here in between fellow forwards Tony Brown and Clive Clark as Tommy Lawrence collects, slotted in the only goal of the game in the 64th minute to point the Baggies towards a relegation escape they eventually achieved with plenty to spare.

FA Cup sixth-round day in late March 1968, and two glimpses of how Albion's FA Cup fate could have been a little different. Geoff Strong holds off Tony Brown's determined challenge (above) to strike a 25-yarder against the top of the Birmingham Road End bar. Also in view are Roger Hunt, Graham Williams, Ian Collard and Jeff Astle. Below: Another uneasy time for Alan Ashman's men as Doug Fraser ushers the ball away from trouble as Roger Hunt closes in. Also offering support to John Osborne are Eddie Colquhoun (a Scottish-born defender who was ruled out of the Wembley reckoning when he injured his ankle in a 2-2 draw at Newcastle in mid-April), Collard and Brown.

John Osborne, watched by John Kaye and right-back Dennis Clarke, clutches safely from Ron Yeats in front of The Kop as the action moves on to Anfield for the replay.

The deadlock is finally broken as the grounded Osborne and Clarke watch Tony Hateley fire home the loose ball. But Albion bounced back thrillingly in a game witnessed by more than 54,000 and levelled with a Jeff Astle header, extra-time bringing no further goals.

John Osborne, Albion's extrovert bird-watching, cricket-loving £15,000 recruit from the famous Chesterfield goalkeeping academy, dives to push wide a Roger Hunt shot in the second replay at Manchester's Maine Road on Thursday, 18 April. On hand just in case is the heroic John Kaye, sporting a bandage because of a first-half cut that required stitches during the game.

Another sign of Liverpool's at-times intense pressure as Jeff Astle joins his goalkeeper to repel a moment of concern near Albion's line. But, despite a first-half equaliser by Hateley to Astle's customary goal, it was Alan Ashman's men who won it thanks to Clive Clark's opportunist effort midway through the second period.

The day that Albion really lorded it over Merseyside! Jeff Astle's sweetly-struck left-foot extra-time shot zips across Everton goalkeeper Gordon West and decides the 1968 FA Cup Final at Wembley. No 7 Graham Lovett and No 10 Bobby Hope, whose request for a transfer became public the very next day, get ready to celebrate the Midlands Footballer of the Year's feat of scoring in every round of the competition.

One very happy group! Back row (from left): Doug Fraser, Dennis Clarke, John Osborne, Tony Brown, Graham Lovett, Jeff Astle, John Talbut. Front: Ian Collard, skipper Graham Williams, Clive Clark, Bobby Hope. Absent from the picture is John Kaye, whose injury had enabled Dennis Clarke to become the first substitute ever to appear in an FA Cup Final – "…a question I've often answered in pub competitions," the defender says.

Cup Specialists

RON Atkinson once said that West Bromwich Albion should erect a monument to Tony Brown in the Hawthorns centre circle for all the magnificent deeds he performed in their colours. By the same token, the club might at various times have thought about striking some kind of honour to the scouts and talent-spotters who netted them such an array of stalwart stars from Scotland and the North-East of England in the 1960s and early 1970s.

Just as a fresh-faced Brown was hauled in from South Manchester Schools out of the clutches of those in power at Maine Road – destined to become the man who delivered 279 goals to the navy blue and white cause – so Albion benefitted from a large number of players who might well have been expected to be snapped up by the likes of Newcastle, Sunderland and Glasgow giants Celtic and Rangers.

Certainly, Albion had no geographical right to raid such distant patches in the way they did; only a good name for giving talented young lads a chance, plus a proud long-time status as an established top-flight outfit.

But in came a stream of little-knowns who were to become stars at The Hawthorns... Bobby Hope, Doug Fraser, Alistair Robertson, Ray Wilson, Asa Hartford and Ken Foggo arrived from north of the border. From just this side of Hadrian's Wall, the welcome mat was put out for Bobby Cram, Ian Collard, Gordon Nisbet and, a few years later, Bryan Robson and John Trewick.

The common thread between the vast majority – Fraser, at £23,000 from Aberdeen in 1963 was an exception – was that they cost nothing in transfer fees and gave sterling service at The Hawthorns.

Of the club's Tartan Army, Robertson made a towering 626 first-team appearances, Hope stacked up 403, Fraser 325, Wilson 284, Hartford 275 and Foggo 136, all having been landed straight from school or from non-League clubs in their homeland.

The North-East connection was every bit as strong. Cram was spotted while playing for Durham Boys and was pulled in prior to turning out in more than 160 Albion first-team games.

Collard's 97 senior games for the club included the 1968 FA Cup Final triumph and the League Cup heartache against Queen's Park Rangers the year before. Nisbet's unusual career, which is given a good airing in the pages of this book, saw him handed 167 senior outings by Albion and several hundred elsewhere, and Trewick was to serve the club in 134 matches and, over several years a decade and a half later, in a coaching capacity.

Then there was Robson, arguably the greatest discovery of the lot. He cut his teeth perfectly and impressively at The Hawthorns before becoming Great Britain's most expensive footballer via the un-popular deal that took him and midfield colleague Remi Moses to Ron Atkinson's Manchester United in 1981 in a package worth £2 million. He was a product of Chester-le-Street Boys and, over 249 inspirational matches, proved very much Albion's gain in the years following his capture after he had had trials with Burnley, Coventry and even one of his local clubs, Newcastle.

Hartford, a left-footed terrier-like midfielder in the Robson mould, also moved on at handsome profit when he joined Manchester City for £225,000 in 1974, three years after a proposed £170,000 move to Leeds had collapsed because a medical suggested he had a hole in the heart.

But, despite these eventual big-money departures, the order of the day was very much one of loyalty, not of hopping from club to club in the manner of today's game.

Albion's Cup Final 11 back in 1968, in fact, was made up entirely of players who served the club over a long period of time – John Osborne (312 games, 11 years), the aforementioned Fraser (325 games, eight years), skipper Graham Williams (360 games, 18 years), Tony Brown (720 games, 20 years), John Talbut (193 games, five years), John Kaye (361 games, eight years), Graham Lovett (156 games, eight years), Collard (97 games, seven years), match-winner Jeff Astle (361 games, ten years), Hope (403 games, 13 years) and Clive Clark (353 games, eight years).

There weren't too many cherry-pickers in that little lot, nor many looking to make a fast buck and to use The Hawthorns as a stepping stone to riches elsewhere. They were Albion men, good and true.

No wonder the dressing-room had a spirit to envy and the club boasted a major fan appeal that was bolstered by the glorious achievement of reaching four major cup finals in just five seasons.

"Just keep it tight for the first 20 minutes or so"... those were the words of manager Jimmy Hagan when Albion headed to Old Trafford for the opening day of 1966-67 – the first day of League football after England's World Cup glory. The plan didn't work. Albion, under threat here from a Denis Law header, were 5-1 down at 3.20pm and were beaten 5-3. Also in the picture are Tony Brown (on the post), Ray Potter, John Kaye, Stan Jones and Graham Williams.

Alarm bells for Albion as a brave dive by Rick Sheppard and a lunge by Stan Jones are called for as Steve Earle shoots goalwards for Fulham at The Hawthorns in the goal-laden but troubled start to 1966-67. Not that this game held too many terrors for Jimmy Hagan's side, who ran out 5-1 victors after winning 3-1 at Newcastle in the midweek. *Picture courtesy of Ken Coton.*

Nervous moments for Albion as they prepare to face a free-kick in the area in the 2-2 draw at Sunderland on 8 October 1966. One of the youngest sides the club have ever put out are represented in the mass wall in front of goalkeeper Ray Potter and Bobby Hope. Forming the barricade are (from left) Ian Collard, Ray Treacy, Doug Fraser, Graham Williams, Campbell Crawford, Danny Campbell and Dick Krzywicki, with Kenny Stephens and Clive Clark on the right.

Albion were embroiled in a relegation scrap when they visited Fulham early in the New Year in 1967, this 2-2 draw, marked by a power cut and the loss of a two-goal lead, doing little to lift their spirits. Graham Williams is pictured tackling Allan Clarke while, in the background are Doug Fraser and John Osborne, the goalkeeper playing his second game for the club following a £15,000 move from Chesterfield.

West Ham were one of the great Cup sides of the mid-1960s, built around the trio of Bobby Moore, Geoff Hurst and Martin Peters, who enjoyed success of a certain international nature in 1966! But the Hammers, having lifted the FA Cup in 1964 and the European Cup Winners' Cup a year later, found Albion too hot in the League Cup. Beaten by Jimmy Hagan's side in the two-leg 1965-66 Final, they also finished a distant second best in this 1966-67 semi-final. Following the Throstles' crushing 4-0 first-leg victory, the issue was rarely in doubt, although Johnny Byrne raised East London hopes with this early shot (above) through a goalmouth packed by (from left) Stan Jones, a falling Rick Sheppard, Hurst, John Kaye, Ian Collard and Doug Fraser. Below: In a second leg that finished 2-2 thanks to goals from Bobby Hope and Clive Clark, there was a reminder for goalkeeper Sheppard of the proximity of the fans at Upton Park as he was poked with flagsticks by young fans.

A watershed FA Cup day. Peter Lorimer slams in one of the goals with which Leeds crushed Albion 5-0 in a fourth-round tie at Elland Road on 18 February 1967. Bobby Cram (No 2), Stan Jones, diving goalkeeper Rick Sheppard and (in the distance) Graham Williams are the Albion players pictured in what still stands as the club's record defeat in the competition. But it was the Throstles' last FA Cup defeat for well over two years.

The ups and downs of Albion's League Cup Final against Third Division QPR in March 1967 – the first time the competition had been concluded at Wembley. Clive Clark, the second highest goal-scoring winger in the club's history, crashes in the first of his two goals before half-time to make history as the first man to score in every round of the competition in one season. The former England Under-21 international, who played for Rangers before and after his eight-year Hawthorns stint of 98 goals in 353 appearances, did, in fact, score in every match of the holders' run, netting in both legs of the semi-final against West Ham.

But the afternoon turned to woe as QPR hit back from two down to win with three goals in the final half-hour, set on their way by this Roger Morgan header. Nearest the scorer is right-back Bobby Cram, the uncle of athlete Steve Cram and a man playing the last of his 163 senior Albion games.

Rick Sheppard, a goalkeeper well versed in the spectacular, arches himself backwards to hang on under fierce pressure from Liverpool's Tony Hateley – father of England striker Mark Hateley – in the First Division clash at The Hawthorns on 2 September 1967. Sadly, Sheppard fell over the line with the ball! Keeping a close eye is defender Eddie Colquhoun. Albion lost 2-0.

Little more than a formality as Tony Brown blasts a penalty past Tommy Lawrence in front of Anfield's Kop on 6 January 1968, Clive Clark, Jeff Astle, Bobby Hope and Tommy Smith not bothering to move in the background. Unusually, Hope, soon to be a full Scottish international, had stepped up for and missed the original kick, only for Albion to be reprieved when a retake was ordered. *Picture courtesy of Liverpool Post and Echo.*

A long, patient wait for the masses as they queue down Middlemore Road near The Hawthorns for tickets for the FA Cup semi-final against Birmingham in April 1968. The backlog caused by Cup progress and replays – two of them against Liverpool in the quarter-final – meant Albion had to play six League games in the first 20 days of April and two more in the four days after the all-West Midlands Villa Park clash.

Little Clive Clark climbs between two opponents to try a first-half header at goal on the late-April day that 60,831 packed into Villa Park for the semi-final showdown between Alan Ashman's Albion and Stan Cullis's Blues. The Second Division underdogs put up a tremendous battle and were unlucky not to score.

Jim Herriott, watched by defender Winston Foster, leaves his line to gather from Jeff Astle as Albion press again while kicking towards the Holte End before half-time.

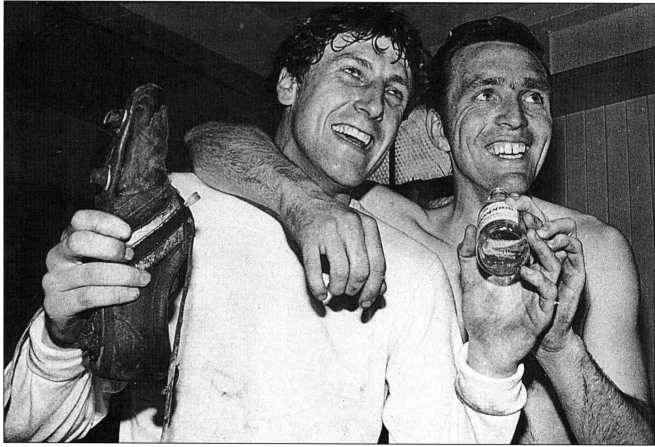

A picture that needs little explanation. Goalscorers Tony Brown and Jeff Astle toast Albion's 2-0 victory at Villa Park on 27 April 1968. Astle's left foot and Brown's right did the damage and saw the favourites through to their third major final in three seasons.

Wembley Wonders

Right, who do this lot support? Ten-year-old Raymond Jackson appears to have a premonition about his club's first FA Cup Final appearance in 14 years as he sets off to Wembley in a party from the West Bromwich butcher's firm Barretts and Baird.

Excited pre-match faces among the Albion contingent, complete with lucky mascots.

Entry of the combatants. Rival skippers Graham Williams and Brian Labone lead the way out.

Gordon West punches clear from a falling Graham Lovett and flying Clive Clark, as Tommy Wright and John Hurst stand by.

John Osborne's safe hands deny Hurst, with Joe Royle racing in just in case of a spill.

Close escape for Albion as Jimmy Husband slices wide of the near post from one of the game's few clear-cut chances. Graham Williams and John Kaye are the covering defenders.

Osborne again in confident mood as he takes control of an attack headed by Royle and Alan Ball and patrolled by Kaye and John Talbut.

Another test for Albion's defence but Talbut and Kaye are up to the task of repelling Hurst and the flying Royle.

New attack, same outcome... Ball, who had scored four goals in Everton's 6-2 League win at The Hawthorns only two months earlier, draws a blank at a cross that is closely watched by captain Williams (near camera). The other Everton man close by is Jimmy Husband.

An opening for Albion as Tony Brown fires off-target when given room to shoot by Hurst and the more distant Brian Labone.

Osborne, protected by Doug Fraser and Kaye, makes sure of his third clean sheet in the triumphant 1967-68 FA Cup run as he leaves Royle disappointed again.

Something to shout about! Jeff Astle, pursued by Clive Clark, runs off the pitch in celebration of a 102nd-minute match-winner that leaves Everton's defenders stunned. It was the striker's ninth goal of the Cup campaign, in addition to the 26 he scored in 40 League games that season. "I was so excited that I never went to bed that night," he confided. "I just talked and walked round London waiting to pick up the first editions of the papers."

It's all yours! Princess Alexandra, booed by Everton fans before kick-off as she chose an all red outfit that was considered too close to the colours of arch-rivals Liverpool, hands the Cup to Graham Williams, watched by a track-suited John Kaye.

And a lasting first look for the masses…

Another shot of the Cup being held aloft as the winners' medals are handed out.

The start of the party… Williams and Cup descend the Royal Box steps, followed by Kaye, Talbut, Collard, Fraser, Brown, Clarke, Lovett, Osborne, Hope, Clark and Astle.

Tired limbs, but happy faces on the lap of honour.

Memories don't come much better than this! The proudest moment in most footballers' careers and even better if you're captain too.

A close-up for the fans. On the far right is Clive Clark, the tenacious Leeds-born left-winger who scored 98 goals in 353 first-team games before his departure back to QPR in 1969. He wasn't considered to be the same force after being badly hurt in the at-times violent tour of East Africa that immediately followed the Final.

Tony Brown, then only 22 and already converted to an attacking right-half, 'milks it' with Albion supporters.

The ritual scenes for the photographers... Clark and Williams are chaired by jubilant team-mates.

Pour me another drop in this cup here! Albion players rejoice in the winners' dressing-room at Wembley, with John Talbut (with towel and cigarette) joined by Tony Brown, skipper Graham Williams, Graham Lovett and a pensive Clive Clark. On the far left is trainer Stuart Williams, the proud holder of 43 Welsh caps, including 33 as an Albion player.

Ready to face the masses all over again! Alan Ashman, John Talbut, Graham Williams and a half-hidden Ian Collard arrive, with their womenfolk, at Birmingham's New Street station en route for their open-top bus tour of the packed streets of West Bromwich.

Above and below: A happy homecoming! The FA Cup is proudly displayed from a platform outside West Bromwich Town Hall by Albion's players and management. The club departed the following day on a stormy six-match end-of-season tour of East Africa, where there was considerable pride in their feat of remaining unbeaten in the face of great hostility.

A Tough Act To Follow

Having done the 1967-68 League double over Manchester City as Joe Mercer and Malcolm Allison's side followed up their 1966 promotion to the top flight by winning the championship at the second attempt, Albion crashed spectacularly in the Charity Shield clash at Maine Road on 3 August 1968. Here, Francis Lee slams in one of City's goals in a 6-1 win, with Graham Lovett, Graham Williams, Ian Collard and John Kaye powerless to intervene.

The Maine Road woe is complete for Albion – unable to play in their lucky white change strip and back in all red – in this, their fourth appearance in the Charity Shield. Francis Lee's shot flashes past Kaye and Williams, the latter having gone in goal when John Osborne suffered a finger injury that was to periodically dog him throughout his career. The injury let in Alan Merrick (left) for a debut as substitute.

Canine 'pause'! An innocent pitch invader stops play during the 0-0 Hawthorns draw against Liverpool on 2 November 1968. It was the clubs' first meeting since their FA Cup epic and provided Alan Ashman's side with a seventh successive game without defeat in an autumn in which they were making good progress in the European Cup Winners' Cup. The weekend before, Albion had drawn 0-0 at a Leeds side destined to win the title for the first time.

Not satisfied with their Charity Shield romp over Albion, League champions Manchester City League handed the same opponents a 5-1 First Division thrashing in November 1968. Stand-in goalkeeper Rick Sheppard is happy to shut Mike Summerbee out on this occasion as John Talbut and Doug Fraser look on. A few days later, Albion slammed Dynamo Bucharest 4-0 to reach the quarter-final of the European Cup Winners' Cup, where they lost to Dunfermline.

Brave intervention from goalkeeper John Osborne, surrounded by Frank Clarke and team-mates John Talbut and John Kaye, as he punches clear in the First Division game at Loftus Road on 28 December 1968. After a poor away run, this 4-0 win – via goals from Ian Collard (2), Dennis Martin and Ronnie Rees – gave Alan Ashman's men some revenge for the club's 1967 League Cup Final defeat against QPR.

A safe start to the FA Cup defence. Jeff Astle sends Kevin Keelan the wrong way to convert a penalty in the routine 3-0 third-round home win against Second Division Norwich in January 1969. It was one of only three spot-kick goals the striker scored for the club, the last of those coming in a Watney Cup Final shoot-out defeat at home to Colchester in 1971.

Problem time for Albion in their 2-1 FA Cup fourth-round win at Fulham on 25 January 1969. Graham Lovett, a leaping John Talbut and Doug Fraser are the covering men but they can't prevent Stan Brown equalising with this first-half header. George Cohen is the Fulham player on the far left. Albion's goals came early and late from Asa Hartford and substitute Ronnie Rees respectively, Hartford's on his FA Cup debut. *Picture courtesy of Ken Coton.*

A few days after Albion's 2-1 FA Cup sixth-round victory at Chelsea, the club were booked in for another quarter-final assignment at Stamford Bridge, this time in the FA Youth Cup. And the result was the same as a side containing Gordon Nisbet (in goal), Jim Holton, Asa Hartford and Len Cantello marched on towards a 6-3 aggregate defeat in the Final against Sunderland. Hartford (No 8) and Holton, both sent off at Roker Park but destined to become Scottish internationals, lead this attack on Chelsea's goal.

Anguish for Jeff Astle as an effort goes narrowly wide of Peter Shilton's goal in the second half of the FA Cup semi-final against Leicester in front of 53,207 fans at Hillsborough on 29 March 1969. Albion's 1-0 KO – their first defeat in the competition in 15 ties – was all the more surprising given that the East Midlanders were relegated from the First Division a few weeks later.

End of the dream. John Osborne is sprawled out in despair near his post after allowing Black Country boy Allan Clarke's shot in the dying minutes to squirm under his body for the only goal of a tie Albion had been confident of winning. Leicester went on to lose 1-0 to Manchester City in the Final while the Throstles' Cup fortunes went into sharp decline, continuing with a late third-round exit against Sheffield Wednesday at Hillsborough the following season.

Goalkeeper Jim Cumbes, signed by Alan Ashman from Tranmere, breathes a sigh of relief as a header from the grounded Alun Evans flies over an unguarded net in Albion's home clash with Liverpool on 27 September 1969. Striker Bobby Graham can't believe it, nor can the helpless Doug Fraser (left) and John Kaye. *Picture courtesy of Liverpool Post and Echo.*

Sickening moment from the same game as Roger Hunt celebrates his side's equaliser seven minutes into injury-time. Jeff Astle and Colin Suggett are the players with hands on hips, Doug Fraser sinks to his haunches. A game marked by Albion goals from Astle and Danny Hegan was followed a week later by more sense of West Midlands injustice at the hands of referee Keith Walker. At neighbouring Molineux, the official sent off Wolves hero Derek Dougan – the stormy prelude to an eight-week ban. *Picture courtesy of Liverpool Post and Echo*.

John Osborne goes down to save at the feet of Geoff Strong during Albion's 1-0 League defeat at Liverpool on 11 January 1969. John Talbut, Roger Hunt, John Kaye, Chris Lawler and Tony Brown wear suitably serious expressions but, in the background, Graham Lovett sees a funny side to it all. Four days later, Albion drew 0-0 at Dunfermline in the away first leg of their European Cup Winners' Cup quarter-final. *Picture courtesy of Liverpool Post and Echo*.

Who would be a goalkeeper? John Osborne goes down in the Wembley mud to save in Albion's 2-1 1970 League Cup Final defeat against Manchester City. Mike Doyle, who was to score City's 58th minute equaliser, is the man shaping up to shoot if the ball pops free while Francis Lee looks on. Alan Ashman's side lost 2-1 despite Jeff Astle's early headed goal.

The glory is Everton's as Alan Whittle's shot rips into the net to seal the Merseysiders' League championship triumph on 1 April 1970, and exact some revenge on Alan Ashman's Albion for Wembley 1968. Unable to prevent a 2-0 defeat at Goodison Park are (from left) Alistair Robertson, John Osborne, Ray Wilson and, in the background, Bobby Hope. Albion had a bruising run-in, leaking a total of 21 goals in their last six away matches and finishing 16th.

Debutant Archie Gemmill goes crashing under the combined challenge of Asa Hartford and No 8 Colin Suggett in Albion's 2-1 First Division win over Derby on 26 September 1970. Looking on are (from left) John Kaye, John Talbut and Alan Merrick, the latter in an unfamiliar No 2 shirt. Suggett had become the club's record buy at £100,000 in the summer of 1969. *Picture courtesy of Derby Evening Telegraph.*

Albion's area is a congested zone as Denis Law threatens in Manchester United's 2-1 home win on 24 October 1970. Alan Merrick takes a tumble as John Talbut closes in and Jeff Astle, No 6 John Kaye and Doug Fraser look on. The other United player is John Fitzpatrick. Albion were in a terrible away run at the time, going an astonishing 16 months without a League win on the road until triumphing famously and controversially at title-chasing Leeds in April 1971.

Alan Ashman's last League match as Albion manager – a 2-0 defeat at sunny Derby on the final day of 1970-71. Ashman, whose defender John Kaye heads clear here as goalkeeper Jim Cumbes covers an attack featuring Roy McFarland and John O'Hare, was sacked in the July, having led the club to FA Cup glory, a European Cup Winners' Cup quarter-final place and a League Cup Final in his four years in charge. Derby hero Dave Mackay retired as a player after this game. *Picture courtesy of Derby Evening Telegraph.*

A meeting of old friends. Defender Eddie Colquhoun, who played 54 games for Albion after being signed from Bury in 1967, was in Sheffield United colours by the time he threatened the Throstles side now managed by Don Howe in this rain-hit 0-0 Bramall Lane draw on 28 August 1971. John Kaye and Lyndon Hughes are pictured challenging in the air while Tony Brown is No 8 for Albion, who became the first team that season to hold the newly-promoted Blades.

Midfielder Len Cantello, who played 369 first-team games during his 12-year Albion stay, holds off Jimmy McGill in a First Division defeat at Huddersfield on 11 September 1971. It was the side's third 1-0 loss in a row and their fourth successive game without a goal. In all, they failed to score in six matches out of seven and eight out of ten.

Jim Cumbes repels with difficulty an aerial challenge from John O'Hare in Albion's backs-to-the-wall 0-0 draw at Derby on 25 September 1971. Looking on are (from left) John Wile, Tony Brown, Archie Gemmill and John Kaye. Kaye and Cumbes made their last Albion starts when the side lost at home to Manchester City a week later – their 360th and 79th appearances respectively. *Picture courtesy of Derby Evening Telegraph.*

Debut day for Alistair Brown, a bargain £61,000 buy from Leicester, as Albion tackle Crystal Palace in The Hawthorns mud on 11 March 1972. The Scottish-born striker scored in this 1-1 draw and also in the following Friday's win at Coventry as his new club nudged towards safety after at one time looking relegation probables.

A header by Alan Durban comes to nothing as Albion defend in depth through Alistair Robertson, John Wile, Asa Hartford and Gordon Nisbet during a 0-0 floodlit draw with Derby on 5 April 1972. Brian Clough's side were heading for the first League Championship title in the club's history and Albion were the only Division One side that season they didn't score against. *Picture courtesy of Derby Evening Telegraph.*

Derby, this time as champions, are again The Hawthorns opposition as Gordon Nisbet heads away from a lunging John O'Hare on 9 September 1972. John Wile, Len Cantello and a partly-hidden Asa Hartford look on during an unlikely 2-1 Albion win – their first League victory of the season, at the eighth attempt. They had scored only three goals in the previous seven matches.

Colin Suggett, converted by Don Howe from a striker to a midfielder, tangles with his Chelsea counterpart Steve Kember during the League clash at Stamford Bridge on 14 October 1972. Albion had won at Crystal Palace in their previous trip to the capital and scored in this game through a Tony Brown penalty, but their 3-1 defeat hinted at a long winter ahead.

John Wile is heavily outnumbered by Wolves players as defender Bernard Shaw finds himself in danger from a high boot in the First Division derby at The Hawthorns on 21 October 1972. Don Howe's side won with a second-half strike by Bobby Gould, who had arrived from Molineux and who scored 19 times in a 60-game League career at The Hawthorns before moving to Bristol City a few weeks after this game.

Human obstacles in the form of Arsenal duo Peter Storey (left) and the late George Armstrong are strewn in Len Cantello's path as he tries to find a way through for Albion in the League game at Highbury on 16 December 1972. Tony Brown's fifth goal in six games failed to stave off a 2-1 defeat in what was already a struggle for survival.

Gordon Nisbet takes the ball out of danger as Hugh MacLean, a distant Ray Wilson and John Wile survey the confusion of a collision between Albion goalkeeper John Osborne and Ipswich striker Trevor Whymark in the First Division game at Portman Road on 17 March 1973. David Johnson is the other Ipswich player on hand in a game his side won 2-0. *Picture courtesy of East Anglian Daily Times and Evening Star.*

The drop is close as a young Peter Shilton blocks a point-blank shot from Asa Hartford after Tony Brown's penalty had been saved in the dying moments of the home game against Leicester on 7 April 1973. Despite Jeff Astle's winner – and two more points against visiting Everton four days later – Albion lost their last four matches and were relegated for only the fifth time in their history.

Life in the Second

RELEGATION in 1972-73 hit West Bromwich Albion hard. But it didn't altogether come as a surprise. The side taken over by Wolverhampton-born Don Howe in the summer of 1971 had flirted with the drop in the former Hawthorns and England right-back's first season in charge, losing seven First Division matches in a row before Christmas and slipping to the bottom of the table.

But successive victories over Liverpool at home and Ipswich away on 27 December and 1 January respectively initiated a revival that was to secure safety well before the end of the season. The relief, however, was brief. Albion, acquiring the image of a defence-minded side in contrast to their cavalier mid and late-1960s reputation, failed to score in their first three League matches of 1972-73 and in two of their next four. The pattern was set.

Goals came a bit more freely in the autumn and early winter but a grim January, followed by an embarrassing 4-0 crash at home to relegation rivals Crystal Palace on 10 February, accelerated a slide towards Second Division status that was confirmed by Manchester City's 2-1 midweek victory at The Hawthorns on 25 April. It was the first time Albion had been out of the top flight since 1949 and only Arsenal and Manchester United of the then First Division could claim a longer stretch of unbroken service among the elite. No wonder it was tough for supporters to be plotting the way to Hull, Millwall and Oxford rather than negotiating the familiar annual routes to Highbury, Old Trafford and Anfield.

Unlike the present day, there was no great dressing-room clear-out and scramble to save wages following relegation. The players who had taken the club down were, by and large, entrusted with the first crack at getting them up again, which meant the nucleus of the squad was still Peter Latchford, Gordon Nisbet, Ray Wilson, John Wile, Alistair Robertson, Len Cantello, Tony Brown, Asa Hartford, Alistair Brown, David Shaw, Lyndon Hughes and Alan Merrick. Jeff Astle's glorious ten years at the club were drawing to a painful, injury-stricken end, though, and it was in attack that Albion failed most seriously.

After a 3-2 opening-day win at Blackpool, they found goals difficult to come by and the resulting drop in entertainment value was marked by a fall in attendances... from 17,898 for the first home match against Crystal Palace to 11,722 against

Bobby Charlton's Preston in mid-September to 11,456 against Orient in mid-April. Albion were on the fringe of the promotion race for much of the campaign – only the top three clubs went up in those pre-play-off days – but they fell away to finish eighth after being crushed by champions-elect Middlesbrough 4-0.

Hopes weren't particularly high for 1974-75, especially when Tony Brown, whose total of seven goals in eight days against Nottingham neighbours County and Forest had been one of the few highlights of the previous winter, expressed his discontent at the club. Robertson found himself on the outside looking in as well and popular keeper John Osborne was even farmed out to Walsall for a spell as he remained very much second choice behind Latchford. Again, Albion flickered as top-three candidates, winning three successive League games in the autumn in a run of five Second Division matches without a goal against – the sort of statistic Howe's critics thought he was most interested in. Four consecutive wins and four more consecutive clean sheets followed in November and December but hopes of the more important target of promotion were ended by a trot of four defeats in five League games in February and March. Attendances had slipped below 10,000 and there were only 7,812 and 8,130 present for the visits of Notts County and Millwall respectively – the two games at the start of April during a week that was to prove Howe's swansong.

In terms of League position (sixth), Albion were to finish closer to going up than the year before, but they were further away in the hard currency of points. They finished eight adrift of third place, the dissatisfaction of fans and directors probably increased by neighbours Villa's runner-up placing behind champions Manchester United. In Howe's wake, Albion turned to the first player-manager in their history.

Johnny Giles represented tremendous value, as a player alone, on the £48,000 that was paid to secure his services from Leeds in the summer of 1975. As a boss, he was inspirational. With a young Bryan Robson feeling his way after being given his debut at York in the first away match of the post-Howe era, Albion recovered superbly from winning only one of their first 12 League and League Cup games of the season. Giles astutely added his Republic of Ireland colleagues

Mick Martin and Paddy Mulligan to his squad and, although Geoff Hurst's purchase from Stoke did not work out, the side developed a possession-based game that took them up the table.

Starting with a 1-0 home victory against Plymouth in mid-October, they won seven Second Division matches out of ten and 13 out of 21, with Giles at the hub of their thoughtful football. Tony Brown had found a new lease of life, John Osborne was on his way to both an ever-present campaign and a club record number of clean sheets and Robertson had reclaimed his No 6 shirt from David Rushbury. The only way was up. Defeats against Bristol City and Charlton in the spring caused a few flutters but Albion finally made it into the top three for the first time in April 1976 – the month in which they actually secured promotion. They won their last three home games in some style and followed up a tense midweek 0-0 draw at Orient with the famous 1-0 victory at Oldham that ended their three years in the Second Division wilderness. They were back in the big time.

Action from Albion's first Division Two game for almost a quarter of a century. Relegation duly came to Don Howe's side in the spring of 1973 and they kicked off the following season with a Tony Brown-inspired 3-2 win at Bloomfield Road despite this shot by Peter Suddaby, watched by Allan Glover and closed down by Lyndon Hughes, the latter playing his first match after an 11-month absence with a kidney problem. *Picture courtesy of Blackpool Evening Gazette.*

Two men from famous football families come face-to-face in Albion's 1-1 home draw against Carlisle on 13 October 1973. Birmingham-born Peter Latchford, whose brothers played together for Birmingham, copes safely under pressure from Frank Clarke, a member of the famous clan of strikers from Short Heath, Willenhall. England Under-23 international Latchford made 104 Albion appearances before doing well at Celtic.

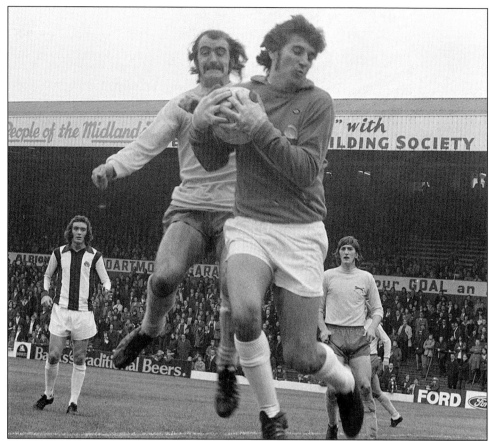

John Wile stays on patrol as a punch by goalkeeper Peter Latchford ends the danger posed by Neil Whatmore and Malcolm Darling as Bolton press in a goalless Hawthorns draw early in Albion's Second Division exile. This 27 October 1973, incident came during the third of four successive clean sheets for Don Howe's side. *Picture courtesy of Bolton Evening News.*

The combined presence of Peter Latchford and John Wile keeps Albion's goal intact on their Second Division trip to Cardiff on 3 November 1973. In the background is Allan Glover, the midfielder who had been bought by Alan Ashman along with Colin Suggett and Danny Hegan in the big-spending summer of 1969. Tony Brown's late strike ensured Albion a 1-0 victory at Ninian Park at the start of a run of four wins in five games. *Picture courtesy of Western Mail & Echo.*

Peter Latchford gathers as Carlisle threaten during Albion's 1-0 win at Brunton Park in March 1974. Willie Johnston's goal gave Albion their first and only victory at the venue in a game played on a Monday afternoon because of the miners' strike and subsequent power cuts. John Wile, Trevor Thompson and Alistair Robertson are the covering defenders while, partly hidden by Thompson, is ex-Albion forward Dennis Martin. *Picture courtesy of Carlisle Evening News.*

Some defending to do for Don Howe's Albion as they sweat over a curled cross from Gary Jones in the 1-1 Second Division draw at Bolton on 9 March 1974. Len Cantello is the player unable to cut out the centre. Albion, who had Jeff Astle making his penultimate start for them, had won at Carlisle and Aston Villa in their previous two games. *Picture courtesy of Bolton Evening News.*

Keeper Peter Latchford loses the ball following a challenge from Bryan 'Pop' Robson in Albion's 1-0 home win over Sunderland on 31 August 1974. Gordon Nisbet and Ally Robertson are the covering defenders as the club register their first points of Don Howe's fourth and final season following opening 1-0 defeats against Fulham and Hull. *Picture courtesy of Newcastle Chronicle and Journal.*

Twice in a month in 1974-75, Albion shut out Bolton at Burnden Park, winning 1-0 there in the League in early December, then drawing 0-0 in this FA Cup third-round tie in the New Year. John Osborne, protected by Gordon Nisbet and a more distant Len Cantello and Joe Mayo, deals safely with a Wanderers threat. *Picture courtesy of Bolton Evening News.*

In the days when Cup replays could be staged three or four days after the original tie, Albion hammered three goals in 13 second-half minutes to blitz Bolton and settle their third-round clash back at The Hawthorns. The slaughter came despite this early shot from Bolton midfielder Peter Reid – now a successful top-flight boss – which troubled (from left) Ray Wilson, Dave Rushbury and John Wile. *Picture courtesy of Bolton Evening News.*

Fifteen months before Albion's travelling masses turned Oldham's Boundary Park into a sea of yellow, green, blue and white on the day promotion was won, there was a much lower-key clash between the sides at the same venue. Left-back Ray Wilson does his ballet impression as Oldham forward Alan Young goes in for a balancing act in a turgid 0-0 draw in Albion's only League game in January 1975. *Picture courtesy of Oldham Evening Chronicle.*

A week after Oldham, Albion slipped out of the FA Cup away to Alan Ashman's Carlisle United – then a top-flight side. Gordon Nisbet scored his first Throstles goal but couldn't prevent an exciting 3-2 fourth-round defeat that contained this melee in the visitors' area. John Osborne lies on the ball while John Wile, Lyndon Hughes and Ray Wilson also take a tumble and Tony Brown, Dave Rushbury and Nisbet keep their feet. *Picture courtesy of Carlisle Evening News.*

The wacky football world of Gordon Nisbet! Albion's North-East-born stalwart, who made his senior debut for the club as a goalkeeper in August 1969, before compiling around 620 League appearances as a full-back in a career that also took in Hull, Plymouth and Exeter, had another brief taste of life between the posts in the Throstles' Second Division game at Sunderland on 1 March 1975. Nisbet took over from a limping John Osborne when, with the score at 0-0, high-riding Sunderland were awarded a 58th minute penalty. Tony Towers, fouled by Allan Glover, smacked the resulting spot-kick against the post, above – much to the relief of a static Nisbet, who was mobbed by his team-mates before he immediately handed the keeper's jersey back to its rightful occupant, below. In front of the *Match of the Day* cameras, though, Albion went on to lose 3-0! Osborne limped off for good near the end and Bob Ward deputised for much of the rest of the season. Nisbet is on the far left of the 'after' picture, which also features Alistair Robertson and a signal for an indirect Albion free-kick from the referee because Towers had headed the rebound over the bar. Nisbet's goalkeeping career had also featured an eventful trip to Roker Park. He was between the posts when Albion lost 6-0 there in the second leg of the 1969 FA Youth Cup Final. *Top picture courtesy of Newcastle Chronicle and Journal. Bottom picture courtesy of Northeast Press Limited, Sunderland Echo.*

Yet another notch on the Tony Brown goal-post, this one an agile header in a 1-1 Second Division draw at Oxford on 15 March 1975. The effort helped make Brown the club's leading League scorer for the fifth successive season and came during the second half of a game in which his side had full-back Ray Wilson sent off.

A landmark Hawthorns occasion on 19 April 1975 – and not just because Willie Johnston ran out for the home game against Cardiff in a clown's mask! The young No 10 is Bryan Robson, lining up for his first senior home game after marking his debut in a 3-1 win at York the week before. Robson, who became one of his country's finest-ever players, scored for managerless Albion against the Welshmen and netted again at Nottingham Forest seven days later.

Right, I want us to have a laugh as well… Johnny Giles (second right) shares a joke with (from left) Bryan Robson, Len Cantello and Ray Wilson following his appointment as manager in the summer of 1975. The genial Irishman, who won 60 full international caps, was the club's first-ever player-boss and was to prove a big hit. *Picture courtesy of Marshall's Sports Service.*

Robson v Robertson. Sunderland's 'Pop' whips a cross round Albion's Ally in the opening weeks of Giles's first Hawthorns reign. This result on 13 September 1975, meant the Baggies had lost 3-0 at Southampton, 4-0 at Fulham and 2-0 at Sunderland in an unpromising first three away League games of the season. The game was the last of north-easterner Gordon Nisbet's 167 appearances for the club. *Picture courtesy of Newcastle Chronicle and Journal.*

A step in the right direction as Albion pick up their first away point and goal under Giles on a grim late-September afternoon at Carlisle. Frank Clarke is left grounded and John Wile covers while John Osborne produces a typically safe catch, watched by Len Cantello and (centre) Geoff Hurst, the World Cup 1966 hero who scored only twice in 12 games for the club after arriving from Stoke. *Picture courtesy of Carlisle Evening News.*

The turning-point game in the promotion season... after picking up only eight points from their first ten League games as well as going out of the League Cup at the first hurdle to Fulham, Johnny Giles's team ended a run of four successive low-scoring Second Division draws by beating Plymouth on 18 October 1975. Willie Johnston, watched by a soon-to-retire Ray Wilson, tries a shot here after Ally Brown had scored the afternoon's only goal. Albion lost just one of their next nine matches – at Plymouth!

Johnny Giles is reunited with his long-time Elland Road midfield partner Billy Bremner on the occasion of the Albion player-manager's testimonial at The Hawthorns on 22 October 1975. A gate of 8,652 saw Leeds beaten 3-1 as the home side were reinforced by some famous names and had Derek Dougan among their goalscorers.

Albion's flourishing season was really rolling when they recorded this 2-1 victory at promotion rivals Bolton in late November. The *Match of the Day* cameras (pictured on the roof of the stand) captured this typically brave intervention by John Osborne, backed up by Ally Robertson and Mick Martin. The recalled Bryan Robson scored a well-taken late winner, Joe Mayo having opened the scoring early on. *Picture courtesy of Bolton Evening News.*

A rare spoke in the works as a pre-Christmas Friday night home game against Southampton brings Albion their first home defeat of the season. Dave Rushbury, a bearded Tony Brown, Alistair Robertson and Alistair Brown are the players repelling this attack in the Saints' 2-0 win, the grounded Rushbury making the 31st and final appearance of a once-promising Hawthorns career. *Picture courtesy of Southern Newspapers Limited.*

Two goals by Tony Brown and one from Ally Brown gave Albion FA Cup revenge for 12 months earlier when they saw off Carlisle 3-1 in a third-round Hawthorns tie in January 1976. They had to come from behind, though, and also survive this penalty appeal when John Osborne challenged Short Heath-born Frank Clarke. Len Cantello is on the line and Mick Martin and Ally Robertson in the background. *Picture courtesy of Carlisle Evening News.*

Albion unleashed their frustration on the training ground after their home game against arch-rivals Bristol City in February 1976, had been called off because of flu in the visitors' camp. Turning on the power against an unusual backcloth are veterans John Wile and John Osborne, pursued by Willie Johnston, Bryan Robson, Alistair Brown, Len Cantello, Joe Mayo, Alistair Robertson, Mick Martin, Johnny Giles, Tony Brown and Paddy Mulligan.

It all went wrong for a while in Albion's game with Blackburn on 13 March 1976 – newly-promoted Rovers' first trip to The Hawthorns for more than ten years. The visitors were two up early on but, partly inspired by Willie Johnston, who is halted here by a fine tackle, Johnny Giles's side rallied for a point thanks to goals by Joe Mayo and John Wile.

Mick Martin tussles with Mick Mellows on 27 March 1976, as Albion secure three more promotion points away to a Portsmouth side who included George Graham and former Liverpool defender Chris Lawler. Victory went the way of Johnny Giles's men thanks to a second-half header by Len Cantello, the result inching ever-present goalkeeper John Osborne closer to what turned out to be a club record of 22 clean sheets in the season.

Closing in on the big time. Ally Brown climbs above his marker in Albion's final home game of their promotion season. This 2-0 win over Nottingham Forest, secured by goals from Mick Martin and Willie Johnston, still left the side with plenty to do in the subsequent games at Orient and Oldham. In the background are Joe Mayo and Martin O'Neill.

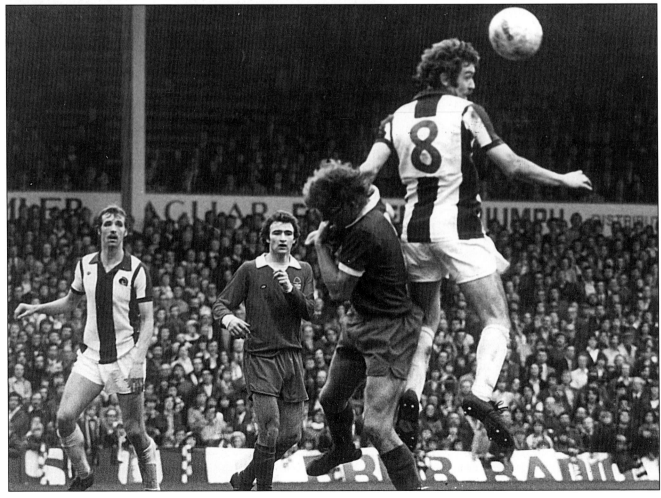

Up, Up and Away

Tense scene from Albion's promotion-clinching victory at Oldham on 24 April 1976, when there were some 15,000 travelling fans in a gate of 22,356. Needing a win to pip Bolton to third place behind Sunderland and Bristol City, they had John Wile and a grounded Johnny Giles looking on here as Len Cantello boots clear in the second half from striker David Shaw, who had played 96 games for Albion and started that season with them. *Picture courtesy of Oldham Evening Chronicle.*

Job done! Albion veteran Bert Millichip, later to become a Sir and an FA supremo, joins in the fun in the away dressing-room at Boundary Park as the club savour the prospect of top-flight football.

The 1-0 win was secured by a second-half left-foot volley by Oldham-born Brown, who is given a smell of the bottle's cork by Joe Mayo as the celebrations start among (from left) Johnny Giles, Alistair Robertson and John Wile. Director Sid Lucas is the man applying the champagne shampoo.

A hero's welcome home. Player-boss Giles is mobbed by supporters as Albion arrive back at The Hawthorns from Oldham. A few weeks later, the brilliant midfielder stunned the club by announcing he was to quit his post, although he was subsequently persuaded to rethink and continue for a second season.

In the same spring that Albion won promotion, their youngsters lifted the FA Youth Cup for the only time in the club's history. Beaten finalists on a 6-3 aggregate against Sunderland in 1969 (despite winning the first leg 3-0!), Albion trounced Wolves 5-0, adding this 3-0 second-leg triumph on 3 May to a 2-0 victory at Molineux. Wolverhampton-born Derek Statham is the player being shut out as Colin Gregson (right) waits for the loose ball.

Saudi Arabia's national side, managed by former Wolves boss Bill McGarry, were more at home than their opponents in the summer heat when they faced Albion in a 1976 training-pitch friendly. Challenging for possession is John Trewick, watched by two strikers who didn't establish themselves at first-team level at The Hawthorns, Ian Edwards (left) and Kevin Summerfield.

Albion's first away win back in the top flight came at neighbours Birmingham on 11 September 1976, when a Tony Brown special did the trick. This was a first top-flight start for Bryan Robson (left), who was still on the fringes of the side as he challenged John Connolly, with Willie Johnston trying to put in a tackle. Incredibly, Robson – then still 19 – broke a leg three times that season.

An unhappy, but newsworthy 90 minutes under The Hawthorns lights. Tipton-born Joe Mayo, nearing the end of a 90-game, 20-goal Albion first-team career, is robbed by Harry Wilson in the shock 2-0 League Cup defeat at home to Third Division Brighton on 22 September 1976. The Baggies' third-round exit from a competition in which they had beaten Liverpool at the previous stage came with a sensational late sending-off, fiery winger Willie Johnston being adjudged to have aimed a kick at the referee!

An occupational hazard of top-flight life in the mid-1970s. All 11 Albion players form a human wall in the face of a Bruce Rioch free-kick in the clash at Derby's Baseball Ground in late September 1976. The message from Johnny Giles as he turns to speak to John Wile (above) is no doubt to remain as a solid line. The wall breaks (below) but the Albion goal was safe this time. However, goals from Roy McFarland earned Derby a 2-2 draw in a game in which Albion had led through two Ray Treacy goals.

A clean catch by John Osborne from a corner in Albion's midweek 2-0 defeat at Newcastle on 6 October 1976. Looking on are Paddy Mulligan, John Wile, Mick Martin, a half-hidden Ally Brown and Ray Treacy. The defeat was sandwiched in between Hawthorns heroics against Tottenham and Manchester United, both of whom had four goals cracked past them. *Picture courtesy of Newcastle Chronicle and Journal.*

Mick Martin strides through the gloom and away from Graham Paddon to slide home in Albion's 3-0 First Division home win over West Ham on 30 October 1976. The Hammers player on the right is Frank Lampard, father of his current namesake at Chelsea. Alistair Brown netted the other two in a game that took Albion's goal tally to 11 in three home matches, Tottenham and Manchester United having been beaten 4-2 and 4-0 respectively.

Portman Road has been the scene of several Albion hammerings, none more emphatic than this 7-0 rout by Bobby Robson's team on 6 November 1976. Trevor Whymark scores past Ally Brown and John Osborne to pile on the agony for Johnny Giles's men. Also pictured are Ally Robertson, John Wile, Ray Treacy, a half-hidden Tony Brown and Len Cantello (almost out of picture), plus Ipswich duo Kevin Beattie and Paul Mariner. *Picture courtesy of East Anglian Daily Times and Evening Star.*

As sick as a dog… Everton defenders are dismayed as No 9 David Cross wheels away to celebrate an extraordinary first goal for the club. The strike came in a 3-0 win on 27 November 1976, an eager Jack Russell terrier having spent around 30 seconds on the pitch, harrying and distracting visiting players in possession, before the ball finally broke for Cross to beat Welsh goalkeeper Dai Davies.

A depressing February night for Albion on Wearside in 1977 as they are crushed 6-1 by a Sunderland side who were still relegated. John Wile appears to be imploring John Osborne to come off his line as the ball breaks towards Bob Lee, who is about to become the victim of a last-ditch Ally Robertson tackle. Lee helped himself to a hat-trick in the rearranged midweek fixture. *Picture courtesy of Newcastle Chronicle and Journal.*

David Cross, who was to score 23 goals in 62 appearances during two spells with Albion, finds himself muscled out of it by Peter Daniel in the 1-0 home win over Derby at The Hawthorns on 5 March 1977. Ally Brown looks on in a clash settled by Bryan Robson's goal. *Picture courtesy of Derby Evening Telegraph.*

Derek Statham and John Wile challenge Sunderland's Mel Holden as Albion head for a pleasing final placing of seventh in the spring of 1976-77. Sunderland won this 30 April clash 3-2 to complete a double over the Throstles, but they were still relegated as Coventry and Bristol City survived in controversial circumstances. Looking on are Johnny Giles and his Republic of Ireland midfield colleague Mick Martin.

Start of a rout – Mick Martin steers a close-range shot past Mark Wallington and Steve Sims to open the scoring for Albion at Leicester on 7 May 1977. The midfielder was capped 52 times for the Republic of Ireland, ten of them while with Albion, and scored again on a day which ended with Johnny Giles's team handsome 5-0 winners. It was one of the club's biggest away victories of modern times.

Sad day for Albion's players and fans as Johnny Giles runs through the guard of honour marking his last home match as Hawthorns player-boss. The genial Irishman, who took over an ailing club in the summer of 1975, had threatened to quit 12 months later after promotion had been won. But, despite his reservations at the manager's lot, he was persuaded to stay another year. Albion marked this May afternoon in style with a 3-1 win against Stoke.

Back on home soil... the livewire Willie Johnston skips a St Mirren challenge in a 4-3 semi-final win in the Tennent Caledonian pre-season tournament in front of more than 40,000 on 6 August 1977. The event was staged at Ibrox Park, where Albion beat hosts Rangers 2-0 in the Final the following day – a sweet return for the winger, who had scored twice for the Scottish giants in the 1972 European Cup Winners' Cup Final in his medal-filled career north of the border.

Derby's Steve Powell takes a tumble as an Albion side under the new control of former Hawthorns legend Ronnie Allen survive in a 1-1 League draw at the Baseball Ground on 15 October 1977. John Wile, Ally Robertson, goalkeeper Tony Godden and Paddy Mulligan are the nervous onlookers. Albion won thrillingly at the venue in the fifth round of the FA Cup in the following February. *Picture courtesy of Derby Evening Telegraph.*

Allen's reign was brief before he defected to become the coach of Saudi Arabia, and John Wile was Albion's caretaker manager over the 1977-78 festive period that included this 3-1 defeat against Arsenal on 27 December at The Hawthorns. Pat Rice is the man sticking out a long leg to block Tony Brown's shot, with Liam Brady, Mick Martin and a half-hidden Bryan Robson looking on. Albion, beaten 3-1 at Bristol City on Boxing Day, appointed Ron Atkinson a fortnight later.

Big Ron

WHERE Johnny Giles articulated with his twinkling feet and the passing game he developed, Ron Atkinson sent out his Albion teams with the orders to entertain him – and then revelled in telling the football world all about how they had done just that!

Giles worked wonders in two years as player-boss at The Hawthorns, lifting a sagging club and leaving them well established in the top flight, only a handful of points short of a surprise place in the UEFA Cup. And there could have been no better man to build on his good work than Big Ron. Under the astute Irishman, Albion had been compact, skilled and successful, the latter to the degree that they followed up third place in Division Two with seventh in Division One – immediately above the distinguished trio of Arsenal, Everton and Leeds. What they certainly weren't was flamboyant. But Atkinson soon saw to that after Ronnie Allen had quickly come and gone for the first of his two managerial stints at The Hawthorns.

Atkinson had a varsity background in the football sense, having played for Oxford and managed Cambridge, and was little-known when chosen as Albion manager in January 1978. But, within months, he was being hailed as one of the game's biggest characters. A thrilling FA Cup journey certainly helped his cause. A side who had already beaten Blackpool in round three were firmly under his command by the time they went to Old Trafford to draw 1-1 in the fourth round and then beat holders Manchester United 3-2 after extra-time in an emotion-sapping replay in the Hawthorns mud.

Atkinson loved those big nights – just how much became clear in 1981 when he found himself unable to resist the lure of United – and had another to savour when Derby were beaten by the same score under the Baseball Ground lights in a delayed fifth-round tie. That conquest over one East Midlands club brought Albion a crack at another, Brian Clough's Nottingham Forest, who at the time were on their way to the Football League championship. Forest were also destined to achieve the magnificent feat of back-to-back European Cup triumphs in that golden era but were no match at The Hawthorns for a side who marched to their first FA Cup semi-final for ten years with goals by Mick Martin and Cyrille Regis.

At the last-four stage, Albion were well fancied to overcome Ipswich, an emerging side managed by former Hawthorns wing-half Bobby Robson. But misfortune with injury, coupled with sudden loss of form, landed them with a sickening Suffolk punch, which Ipswich claim had been inspired by the sight of Atkinson being pictured with the FA Cup on TV that Saturday lunchtime. Failure at the last hurdle before Wembley had the consolation of European qualification through the League, Albion finishing sixth thanks to a last-day draw at home to Forest. And how Big Ron loved his travels round the Continent!

Following a pioneering end-of-season tour of China and Hong Kong, Albion took on and easily beat Galatasaray and Valencia – what would those triumphs mean today? – and underlined their commitment to attacking football as they also went to Portugal and beat Sporting Braga 2-0 en route for a 3-0 aggregate success. In the League, the side were flourishing, winning their first three matches and scoring 12 goals in another golden trio of First Division fixtures against Leeds, Coventry and Manchester City. Five wins and a draw in the next six League games had Albion up near the top of the table and they became genuine title contenders when they won thrillingly on two massive stages immediately after Christmas – 2-1 at Arsenal and 5-3 at Manchester United in a game still revered even by the neutrals who have seen TV footage of it.

Top spot was theirs when they drew at frosty Norwich in mid-January and, around the likes of Laurie Cunningham, Derek Statham, Bryan Robson, Len Cantello, Brendon Batson, Regis and the two Browns, some of their football was truly scintillating. Sadly, it didn't last because 1978-79 was Britain's worst winter in well over a decade and the high-tempo performances ran aground on the heavy pitches of the final three and a half months. Liverpool were the main rivals for the title and they were fortunate to avoid the same sort of enforced activity that had Albion in a ring-rusty state going into the Anfield head-to-head of the top two at the start of February. In front of more than 52,000, Atkinson's men lost 2-1 and then did the same at home to Leeds after another three-week break.

The challenge was revived by six straight League wins but an FA Cup fifth-round replay defeat at Southampton was followed by unlucky UEFA Cup quarter-final elimination against Red Star Belgrade. That left just the championship to go for and, although Albion reeled off four more victories on the trot, they were denied even runners-up place when Trevor Francis's goal in front of the Birmingham Road End in the last match of the season gave Nottingham Forest the honour instead. It was a heart-breaking end to Albion's most impressive campaign since they had almost won the League and FA Cup double in 1954 and was followed by the break-up of the team, Cantello and Cunningham going to Bolton and Real Madrid respectively and Brown ending his 20-year Hawthorns association a few months later.

Although Gary Owen and Peter Barnes proved good signings, David Mills flopped and John Deehan was no more than a moderate success. The result was a disappointing tenth place in 1979-80, and even fourth spot the following year and UEFA Cup qualification came at a high price. Ron Atkinson had developed a glowing reputation in the game and was enticed north by the glamour of Old Trafford. With him went most of Albion's hopes of remaining up with the English elite.

Just over a month prior to their FA Cup semi-final clash – and before resolving their respective quarter-finals – Albion and Ipswich fought out a 2-2 League draw at Portman Road. Two goals by Tony Brown, on the ground where he had made his debut in 1963 at the age of 17, earned a 2-2 draw for Ron Atkinson's side. Willie Johnston is pictured taking on Russell Osman and George Burley while Derek Statham waits in vain for a pass!

Happy Hawthorns scenes at the end of Albion's 2-0 FA Cup quarter-final victory over Nottingham Forest on 11 March 1978. Goals by Mick Martin and Cyrille Regis saw off Brian Clough's men, who were to win the League championship that spring in their first season after promotion – and also lift the European Cup in both of the following two years. Willie Johnston and Dave Needham (almost out of picture) are the players shown leaving the pitch.

Doing their bit for a worthy cause… skipper John Wile leads the Albion dressing-room in signing kidney donor cards four days before the FA Cup semi-final against Ipswich at Highbury. Also pictured are (from left) Willie Johnston, Alistair Robertson, Mick Martin, Cyrille Regis and Laurie Cunningham, with Derek Statham in the background.

Albion's miserable FA Cup semi-final clash with underdogs Ipswich at Highbury in the spring of 1978. A fit and able John Wile is watched by long-time colleague Alistair Robertson and referee Clive Thomas as he challenges 1976 Albion target Paul Mariner. But Wile suffered a bad cut in a clash with Brian Talbot – later to become Hawthorns boss – in trying to prevent the East Anglians' early first goal in their 3-1 victory.

John Wile needed attention from physio George Wright as Tony Godden and Paddy Mulligan shared the skipper's anxiety. Tony Brown scored Albion's goal from a second-half penalty but a Cup journey that had accounted for Blackpool, Manchester United, Derby and Nottingham Forest ended disappointingly short of Wembley. *Pictures courtesy of East Anglian Daily Times and Evening Star.*

Paddy Mulligan lifts some of the post-Highbury gloom as he makes Newcastle suffer with the only League goal of his 132-game Albion career. This strike, witnessed at close quarters by Ally Brown, an appealing Alan Kennedy and Irving Nattrass, secured a 2-0 victory four days after the semi-final but the Dubliner's days were already numbered after the signing of Brendon Batson. Mulligan was a hit under Johnny Giles but new boss Ron Atkinson said: "I simply loathed the fella. Seeing him leave made my day!"

Not yet! Tony Brown was one goal short of Ronnie Allen's all-time Albion record of 208 in the League when he went close with this header in The Hawthorns clash with Bolton on 26 August 1978. Tony Dunne, Manchester United's 1968 European Cup Final left-back, is the closest covering defender. 'Bomber' didn't score in this 4-0 win – his side's third in a row – but equalled Allen's mark at Chelsea on 30 September and passed it at Leeds a fortnight later.

Alistair Brown gets the better of Liverpool left-back Alan Kennedy in a 1-1 League draw at The Hawthorns on 23 September 1978. It was the start of an unlikely head-to-head battle between the two clubs for the title, but the game featured a bizarre and costly equaliser after Laurie Cunningham had fired Albion ahead. Tony Godden went to sleep when rolling the ball towards the edge of his area and a lurking Kenny Dalglish nipped from behind him to score.

The days when Turkish giants Galatasaray were no match for Albion! Laurie Cunningham scores from the spot in a 3-1 second-leg win in the first round of the 1978-79 UEFA Cup. Cunningham had been on target twice when Albion also won 3-1 in the away game, which was played in the Aegean port of Izmir, 200 miles from Galatasaray's base in Istanbul, due to crowd trouble.

Let the good times roll! Coventry substitute Alan Green is kept in check by Derek Statham, John Wile and Bryan Robson in the Sky Blues' 7-1 crushing at The Hawthorns on 21 October 1978. Also pictured in Coventry's unusual chocolate brown change strip are Ian Wallace and Mick Ferguson. The win, in which Statham scored his side's final goal, came early in Albion's 19-game unbeaten run in League and cups. *Picture courtesy of Coventry Evening Telegraph.*

Mike Channon is powerless to intervene as Cyrille Regis, all power and poise, crashes a shot at Manchester City's goal in an exciting clash at Maine Road on 28 October 1978. The striker, signed by Ronnie Allen for a £5,000 pittance, missed out with this effort but netted along with Bryan Robson to earn his side a 2-2 draw. It was one of 17 goals Regis scored in a season that ended with him being named PFA Young Player of the Year.

Alistair Robertson is in control in the routine second leg of Albion's UEFA Cup disposal of Portuguese outfit Sporting Braga on 1 November 1978. An Ally Brown goal gave Ron Atkinson's men a 1-0 win and 3-0 aggregate third-round success after Cyrille Regis's brace in the away leg. Robertson played all 12 games in which Albion appeared in European competition from 1978 to 1981.

Four days before their memorable UEFA Cup draw in Valencia, Albion ground out a 1-0 victory in the less exalted surrounds of rainy Burnden Park. Bolton were struggling at the time but Albion hearts were still in their mouths when John Wile emerged unpunished for this penalty-area challenge on Alan Gowling. This game was the last of Republic of Ireland international Mick Martin's impressive 115-game stint for the club. *Picture courtesy of Bolton Evening News.*

Ally Brown is on his knees and Laurie Cunningham equally disbelieving as Aston Villa's goal survives in the 1-1 draw at The Hawthorns on 25 November 1978. John Gidman, Jimmy Rimmer and John Gregory are the relieved men in a game in which Tony Brown scored from a penalty for the 50th time for the club. Three nights earlier, Cunningham had played brilliantly in Valencia and alerted Real Madrid to his talents. They bought him for an Albion record of £995,000 the following summer.

December 1978 was the best month Albion have had in the last quarter of a century, complete with five wins out of five – the fourth of them this 2-1 Boxing Day win at Arsenal. At the time, Ron Atkinson's side, who won famously at Manchester United (5-3) four days later, were pushing hard for the First Division title and cutting a goal-scoring swathe through Europe. Here, Ally Brown is ready to pounce as Laurie Cunningham wins a header against Willie Young.

Cyrille Regis drives in the goal that shot Albion to the top of the table on 13 January 1979. On a bitterly cold day on which much of the English programme was frozen off, Norwich had Justin Fashanu making his debut. But it was Martin Peters who restricted Albion to a 1-1 Carrow Road draw, his headed equaliser coming while right-back Brendon Batson was off the field because of a problem with his boots!

The goals continued to flow when Coventry found no answer to some inspired attacking in this FA Cup third-round replay in January 1979. They were beaten 4-0 despite this challenge on goalkeeper Tony Godden by Garry Thompson – later to join Albion. The tie was notable for Brendon Batson (pictured foreground), the Grenada-born full-back scoring one of only two goals he managed in 220 Baggies appearances. *Picture courtesy of Coventry Evening Telegraph.*

A replacement for Bomber? David Mills was meant to be pushing Tony Brown on the pitch as well after being signed by Ron Atkinson from Middlesbrough early in 1979 for what was then a British transfer record fee of £516,000. But the former England Under-21 international flopped at Albion, where he scored only six goals in 76 senior appearances.

A terrific left-foot strike from John Wile puts Albion one up in extra-time in the replay of their FA Cup fourth-round clash with Leeds on 26 February 1979. Ally Brown completed a 2-0 win for a Baggies side who staged both clashes as Leeds were banned from playing home ties. The teams had drawn 3-3 earlier in the week, with the Yorkshiremen winning 2-1 in the League at The Hawthorns just prior to that. Incredibly, the clubs also met three times in the 1978-79 League Cup and Wile played 75 of the 76 first-team fixtures (including friendlies) Albion fulfilled that season – the highest by any player in the club's history.

The small matter of 391 Albion goals between them, Tony Brown (279) and Cyrille Regis (112) take a breather during training before the first leg of the UEFA Cup quarter-final tie against Red Star in Belgrade on 7 March 1979. Atkinson's men were beaten 1-0 by a late free-kick in a game watched by a massive 95,300.

More full-blooded commitment from John Wile as he lunges in to block as Ian Wallace and Alan Green threaten in Albion's 3-1 First Division win over Coventry in the Highfield Road mud on 3 March 1979. Also pictured is David Mills, who scored along with Bryan Robson and Ally Brown, in what was his first League start for the club after two substitute appearances. *Picture courtesy of Coventry Evening Telegraph.*

The time when Albion's triple pursuit of honours started to creak. A heavy backlog of fixtures, caused both by Britain's severest winter for many years and by UEFA Cup and FA Cup progress, began to take its toll when Southampton arrived at The Hawthorns on FA Cup fifth-round day. Atkinson's men, in animated protests with the officials through the defensive rocks of Ally Robertson and John Wile, were held to a 1-1 draw on a sapping pitch.

Despite a Laurie Cunningham goal, Albion were beaten 2-1 in extra-time in the replay at The Dell only two nights later, when Robertson slides in on Terry Curran, watched by Wile, Brendon Batson and Phil Boyer. Albion had to cram in eight games in March, the same in April and six in the first 18 days of May. *Pictures courtesy of Southern Newspapers Limited.*

Laurie Cunningham does battle with a well-known 21st century Black Country face on another quagmire of a Hawthorns surface on 7 April 1979. Ally Brown was the scorer on what was Martyn Bennett's Football League debut – a game in which Albion made it six League wins in a row. The opponent? Dave Jones, then of Everton and more latterly manager of Wolves.

With the mud giving way to more traditional spring pitches, Albion were buckling under the sheer weight of games by the time they faced visiting Wolves on 21 April 1979. Bryan Robson's goal, scored despite the efforts of Kenny Hibbitt and a grounded George Berry, raised their hopes but an equaliser from their rivals meant they had gone six matches without a win – one of them lost, all the others drawn 1-1 – and handed the initiative to Liverpool in the title race.

One for the Bomber scrapbook... Tony Brown receives his third Midland Footballer of the Year award on 5 May 1979. The presentation was made before Albion's 1-0 home victory against Manchester United by the legendary Matt Busby, a hero to a player born in Oldham and raised in Manchester as a Stretford Ender. Manchester City tried to sign him in 1961, only to be left disappointed by the lure of Albion. "There was something about The Hawthorns," he said. "I just took to it straightaway."

A heartbreak finish... Albion's outstanding 1978-79 season eventually left them in third place after they had lost 1-0 in both this last away game of the season (at Tottenham) and in their final home game (against runners-up Nottingham Forest). There's no way through here for Ally Brown and David Mills as Spurs' Colin Lee closes in.

Albion narrowly survive the double threat of Willie Morgan and Alan Gowling in their 0-0 draw at Bolton on 8 September 1979. Tony Godden, Derek Statham and John Wile are the anxious covering men on an afternoon when the home No 10 was Len Cantello, who had just moved back to his native Greater Manchester. *Picture courtesy of Bolton Evening News.*

Alistair Robertson powers a header towards the Manchester City goal as Albion's stuttering start to 1979-80 gives way to a crushing 4-0 home win on 15 September. The rugged central defender is one of the long-time fixtures in Hawthorns history, making his debut against Manchester United in 1969 and ten years later passing Jimmy Dudley's record of 166 consecutive League appearances for the club. His final appearance tally in competitive games was 626.

Alan Hansen looks almost rattled as an also-grounded Cyrille Regis, joined in attack by Gary Owen, presses in the First Division clash with Liverpool at The Hawthorns on 29 December 1979. But Phil Thompson is about to go to the rescue and the then invincible Merseysiders won 2-0 en route to retaining the League championship crown they had lifted despite Albion's memorable challenge the year before.

Cyrille Regis stoops as team-mate Gary Owen floats a header towards goal in the FA Cup third-round clash with West Ham in January 1980. It was Regis, though, who struck late to earn Albion an Upton Park replay, which they lost 2-1 to the eventual Cup winners despite the last of Tony Brown's 279 competitive goals for the club.

Before the changeover... Garry Thompson joined Albion in 1983 and Cyrille Regis moved to Coventry in 1984, but they are captured here playing for their first clubs during the Baggies' 2-0 First Division win at Highfield Road on 8 March 1980. Also in shot in a game won by two Peter Barnes goals are (from left) Remi Moses, Bryan Robson, John Wile, Brendon Batson and Alistair Robertson. The players are wearing black arm-bands following the death of veteran Football League official Alan Hardaker. *Picture courtesy of Coventry Evening Telegraph*.

The changing face of The Hawthorns – the half-demolished old Halfords Lane Stand is the backdrop as Albion press Arsenal's goal through John Deehan, John Wile and Peter Barnes on the opening day of the 1980-81 campaign. In the frame for a Gunners side who won 1-0 are Frank Stapleton, John Hollins, David O'Leary and David Price.

Plenty to smile about for Alistair Robertson and two Preston players as they leave the field after a 1-1 Deepdale draw in a League Cup fourth-round replay draw in November 1980. Barry Cowdrill is the other player pictured from an Albion side who won the second replay 2-1 at The Hawthorns, only to go out at Manchester City in the next round.

Easy does it! Former Manchester City midfielder Gary Owen sends Gary Bailey the wrong way with a penalty to set Albion on the way to a 3-1 victory over Manchester's other team in front of the *Match of the Day* cameras on 27 December 1980.

Following on from the previous page's picture, Albion's second goal came from another ex-Maine Road star Peter Barnes before, with this prodigious leap, Cyrille Regis hurtles over the shoulder of Manchester United centre-half Graeme Hogg and heads the killer third. Ron Atkinson's side had drawn 0-0 at Sunderland the day before.

Vintage Cyrille Regis! Albion's great striking find of the late 1970s is all poise and power as he launches a header at Ray Clemence's goal during the 2-0 home victory over Liverpool on 7 February 1981. This header didn't go in but Regis still scored, along with Bryan Robson, against a side who were taking a year off from winning the title after being crowned champions for four of the previous five seasons. The covering player is Graeme Souness.

A big 4 April win for Albion, 3-1 over Bobby Robson's Ipswich, who were pushing hard for the League championship. Cyrille Regis is denied here by Black Country-born goalkeeper Paul Cooper as John Wark and Bryan Robson look on but goals by the three Bs – Brown (Ally), Batson (his only one in 172 League games for the club) and Barnes kept The Hawthorns bubbling.

Albion qualified for Europe once more as they finished fourth in 1980-81 behind third-placed Arsenal, runners-up Ipswich and champions Aston Villa. Their season ended with this goalless midweek draw at Leeds, where John Lukic is seen collecting under pressure from Ally Brown. The game was the last of Peter Barnes's 77 League appearances for the club (23 goals) before he moved to Elland Road.

Bryan Robson displays the London Supporters Branch's Albion Player of the Year trophy on 4 May 1981. The world-class midfielder, who went on to play 90 games for England, win many of the game's top honours and become an OBE, receives this particular prize from John Wile before the centre-half's testimonial game against an International Select X1 in front of a 6,960 gate. A few months later, Robson had gone to Manchester United for a Hawthorns record fee of £1.5m, having played 249 Baggies games and scored 46 goals.

Start of the Slide

July 1981 – and Ronnie Allen works with Tony Godden on the first day of his second spell as Albion manager. Allen took over from Ron Atkinson, but his appointment wasn't great news for the keeper. After a club record 228 consecutive appearances out of what was to be a total Baggies career of 329 games, Godden was dropped for the visit to Tottenham the following October and spent six months out of the side behind local boy Mark Grew. White Hart Lane played a big part in the Kent man's Hawthorns career. He made his debut there in March 1977, and it was also the scene of his last outing for the club in March 1986.

Hawthorns favourites of old are seen on both sides of the divide in this goalless first-leg of Albion's League Cup semi-final against Tottenham on 3 February 1982. Derek Monaghan wins the header against Chris Hughton while No 4 Andy King looks on, along with Garth Crooks and Ossie Ardiles. The game was marred by sendings-off for Martin Jol and Tony Galvin, Spurs winning the second leg 1-0 – their first win in seven meetings with Albion.

Cyrille Regis scored 112 goals for Albion in 302 games and, from day one, displayed a flair for the spectacular. But none of his strikes were hit with more venom than this acclaimed Goal of the Season in the fifth round of the FA Cup at home to Norwich on 13 February 1982. Fittingly, it was the match-winner and put his side through to a quarter-final tie with Coventry, who were also despatched before QPR subjected Ronnie Allen's side to a surprise semi-final KO.

No way through for Albion in their mid-March 0-0 First Division draw at Southampton in a 1981-82 season in which they reached both domestic Cup semi-finals but also flirted with relegation. But the Dell deadlock is not for want of trying as Cyrille Regis and John Wile call the shots in front of an expectant Andy King.

Six years to the day after winning at Oldham and sealing promotion, Albion were left in relegation danger by a 3-2 home defeat against Sunderland that came despite this early goal from Ally Brown. The striker, supported here by Steve Mackenzie and Andy King, scored only three times in 25 League appearances that season and this was Albion's seventh successive League defeat in a season in which they lost in the semi-finals of both major domestic cups.

The Victoria Ground echoed to chants of 'Leeds are down' when Stoke and Albion met on a Thursday night at the very end of the 1981-82 season. Stoke's 3-0 win made them safe and sent the Yorkshire club down instead. Albion, represented here by Steve Mackenzie in a clash with Peter Hampton, Paul Bracewell and Denis Smith (playing the last of his 407 League games for the Potters), had guaranteed their own survival by beating Leeds two nights earlier. Smith later became Albion's manager.

High Molineux survival stakes as Wolves and Albion meet on 1 May 1982, in front of only 19,813. Alistair Robertson, later to move across the Black Country, heads clear from Mel Eves while Gary Owen looks on during a game Albion won 2-1 with goals by Cyrille Regis and Derek Monaghan. Tony Godden, recalled for his first League game in six months, was another hero with an early penalty save from Wayne Clarke. Albion stayed up, Wolves went down.

Goals were in extremely scarce supply around the time Albion, by now in a stripe-less change strip and under the management of Ron Wylie, visited Kenilworth Road on 5 March 1983. Despite the endeavour of Luton's Brian Horton, carefully watched by Peter Eastoe (left) and Gary Owen, this was the side's fourth successive 0-0 draw.

End of the line for long-time Albion No 5 and skipper John Wile, who is flanked by Nicky Cross, Clive Whitehead and Martin Jol as he fails to cut out a shot in the 1-1 draw at Sunderland on 14 May 1983. Wile, born just down the road from his former club at Sherburn in County Durham, was playing his 500th and final League match for the Baggies in a 13-year span in which he missed only 25 League games. His career was also marked by an astonishing 119 Cup outings, confirming him as the club's third highest appearance-maker of all time behind Tony Brown (720) and Ally Robertson (626). *Picture courtesy of Northeast Press Limited, Sunderland Echo.*

A happy start in the sun as Albion players (from left) Martyn Bennett, Garry Thompson, Romeo Zondervan, Alan Webb, Ken McNaught, Martin Jol, Clive Whitehead and Nicky Cross mob Cyrille Regis after his goal in a thrilling opening-day derby at Aston Villa on 27 August 1983. Despite his strike in front of the Holte End, though, Albion lost 4-3.

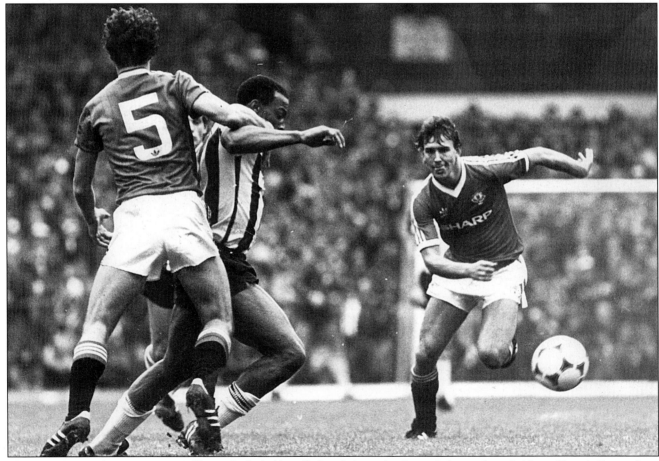

Team-mates turned opponents... Cyrille Regis finds himself closed down by Bryan Robson after shaking off a challenge from Manchester United centre-half Kevin Moran on Albion's visit to Old Trafford on 15 October 1983. This 3-0 defeat came in the latter stages of Ron Wylie's spell as Hawthorns boss and was followed a few months later by Regis's departure to Coventry following a record of 112 goals in 302 Baggies appearances.

Paul Barron leaves his line to gather safely under the watchful eye of Garry Thompson and Romeo Zondervan as No 2 Clive Whitehead feels confident enough to turn his back on the soaring keeper. Albion lost 1-0 in this League game at West Ham on 21 January 1984 but Barron was an ever-present that season and the second half of the 1982-83 campaign in amassing 73 first-team appearances for the club.

Another Old Trafford beating for Albion, this one by 2-0 in the First Division on 2 February 1985, despite a determined leap by Steve Mackenzie between Manchester United defenders John Gidman and Kevin Moran. Also pictured are Gordon Strachan and Garry Thompson. The game was the only one in League and Cup that season in which Tony Godden didn't play, his place in goal going to Paul Barron.

Bruce Grobbelaar, once on The Hawthorns books, fumbles under pressure from Martyn Bennett and Garry Thompson on Liverpool's visit to Albion on 23 March 1985. Steve Hunt is also on hand but the then conquering Merseysiders didn't have to worry. After an early-season 0-0 draw between the clubs at Anfield, they won 5-0 – one of the heavier home defeats in Albion's history.

Going Down

A rare moment to savour during Albion's desperate relegation season of 1985-86. Martyn Bennett is buried by Mickey Thomas, George Reilly, Imre Varadi, Steve Hunt and Derek Statham as they celebrate the only goal of the 8 February derby at a snowy St Andrew's. The victory was one of only four by Albion in the League, one of the other three coming against a Birmingham side who also went down that season. Des Bremner is the dejected defender on a day when the home goalkeeper was David Seaman.

Albion's last game in the top flight for more than 15 years... Paul Dyson is denied by a punched clearance from Black Country-born Phil Parkes in West Ham's 3-2 victory at The Hawthorns on 3 May 1986. Grounded and hoping for pickings are No 7 Martin Dickinson and George Reilly, the striker who went down as the last goalscorer of the club's ten-year First Division stay by converting a penalty after Craig Madden had also netted.

Aerial combat during Albion's goalless draw at promotion-bound Aston Villa on 18 December 1987. Stuart Gray climbs highest, with the balding George Reilly challenging and Steve Lynex (No 6), Carlton Palmer (half-hidden) and Don Goodman the other Albion players pictured. Lynex was in his second spell at the club, having failed to make a senior outing during his 1974-77 stint.

Stewart Phillips and Gary Robson celebrate one of Albion's goals in a 4-1 victory at Birmingham on 15 October 1988, the day Brian Talbot was appointed manager. The former England midfielder was initially caretaker boss following the departure of Ron Atkinson for the second time and was upgraded during a winter marked by promise of a promotion challenge. Phillips, Robson and ex-Blues man Robert Hopkins were on target at St Andrew's.

Gary Robson turns away in delight and Don Goodman moves towards a somersaulting Colin Anderson, who has just given Albion the lead at Chelsea in the Second Division clash on the last day of 1988. There's a particular look of disbelief on the face of Graham Roberts, whose deflection provided a useful 'assist'. But the defender, who moved to The Hawthorns in 1990, scored a last-minute penalty equaliser to keep Chelsea top and Albion second.

Albion's top spot in Division Two is confirmed as they register a 4-0 Hawthorns romp against Shrewsbury on 2 January 1989. Powerless to intervene in this determined goalmouth challenge by Gary Robson is No 5 David Moyes – Preston's highly-rated manager at the time of the 2000-01 play-off campaign. He scored an own-goal in a win that took Albion's record under Brian Talbot to 33 points from 14 League games. But things soon went wrong.

Carlton Palmer (left) waits for an Albion corner in the last of his 139 senior appearances for the club – a 2-0 League defeat at Bradford on 18 February 1989. Palmer was sent off in this game, as was Robert Hopkins, and joined Ron Atkinson's Sheffield Wednesday soon after. The fixture was a significant one for the other two Albion men in shot. Don Goodman was present at the Valley Parade fire of 1985 and Kevin Bartlett (rear) was making his debut. On the far right is Paul Jewell, who managed Bradford City to the Premiership in 1998.

How did that one stay out? Colin West and Don Goodman hold their heads in disbelief as Sheffield United's goal remains intact during the Blades' 3-0 Hawthorns triumph on the first day of the 1989-90 (old) Second Division campaign. Brian Talbot appears to find the misfortune a shade easier to take. It was the 11th time in a row that Albion had failed to win on the opening day of a campaign.

Stuart Naylor gathers from Mark McGhee during Albion's 1-0 Littlewoods Cup third-round victory at Newcastle on 25 October 1989. Chris Whyte (left) scored for a side who were beaten 2-0 at Derby in round four. Micky Quinn, Colin Anderson, Simeon Hodson and (on the far right) 1991 Albion signing Wayne Fereday are also pictured. *Picture courtesy of Newcastle Chronicle and Journal.*

A week after their impressive victory at St James's Park, Albion collapsed against Newcastle in a League game back at The Hawthorns. The visitors raced to a 5-1 victory in a game marked by Sam Allardyce's only competitive senior game for Albion. The Dudley-born player-coach, the manager who led Bolton to their play-off win over the Baggies in May 2001, is wearing No 14 as a substitute as he leads this assault on Newcastle's goal.

One that didn't go in! Chris Whyte and substitute John Thomas watch an effort bounce back off the bar on the day Albion slammed Barnsley 7-0 on 11 November 1989. In the same month, Brian Talbot's team lost 5-1 at home to Newcastle in the League and 5-0 at home to Derby in the Zenith Data Systems Cup. Don Goodman scored a hat-trick against Barnsley and became the first Albion player since Tony Brown in 1970-71 to score 20 League goals in a season. This romp was Martyn Bennett's last game for Albion.

The slogan on the roof of the stand was questionable when Albion faced Swindon in a Sunday clash eight days before Christmas 1989. Angry Brian Talbot fined Bernard McNally for missing this penalty but stopped short of handing the same punishment to Graham Harbey, who blazed a second spot-kick over the bar. McNally's offence: Placing his shot, not 'driving' it. In a bizarre game, Don Goodman scored past Fraser Digby from a third penalty in the space of six sensational minutes but Ossie Ardiles's Swindon still won 2-1.

When things looked promising... Tony Ford, who was to go on to take his tally of Football League appearances towards 900 in a career spanning nine clubs, is congratulated by Gary Bannister (left) and Don Goodman after the goal that earned Albion a point at Portsmouth on the opening day of 1990-91. The 1-1 draw was a decent start to a campaign which ended in five more 1-1 draws for the club – and relegation.

Gary Bannister enjoyed facing Notts County in 1990-91. He stretches here to slide in one of the two goals he scored in a 4-3 defeat at Meadow Lane on 10 November and came up with another brace when the clubs drew 2-2 at The Hawthorns in late February. Bannister scored 20 goals in 81 appearances for Albion after being bought from Coventry and returned to Nottingham when he joined Forest in 1992.

Injury robbed Albion of the services of Don Goodman for more than half of 1990-91 – and the outcome might have been totally different had the striker stayed fit. He still scored eight League goals, including this twisting header in a 2-2 draw on 6 April away to Wolves, the club he was to join from Sunderland in December 1994. Andy Thompson, once of Albion and pictured next to the referee, was the Wanderers left-back on the day Tony Ford was the visitors' other marksman.

Paul Williams works hard to keep his balance at Bristol Rovers' borrowed home ground at Twerton Park, Bath, as he challenges for a high ball in Albion's fateful final game of the 1990-91 season. But the striker was never a success at The Hawthorns and was part of the side who were relegated to the lower divisions for the first time in the club's then 112-year history after a 1-1 draw that ended in tears on the terraces and in the directors' box. *Picture courtesy of Bristol Evening Post.*

A rare shot of Ugo Ehiogu in Albion colours. The powerful defender is pictured (second left) with (from left) Colin West, Dave Pritchard, Adrian Foster and Wayne Dobbins as Albion show off the Birmingham Senior Cup after beating Nuneaton in 1991. Ehiogu played only two senior games for the club – both as substitute in 1990-91 – before being snatched away by neighbours Aston Villa. But a modest tribunal-fixed fee included a precious sell-on clause that netted Albion a further £3m when the England international moved to Middlesbrough in 2000-01 for £8 million.

Welcome to the Football League's lower reaches! Tony Ford keeps team-mate Don Goodman out of possible danger as tempers flare in Albion's first-ever game in the lower divisions. It was a culture shock for the club and their fans to be going to Hartlepool, Darlington and Chester. At least this starter against Exeter in August 1991, resulted in a 6-3 victory.

It's a whole-hearted Hawthorns farewell for Don Goodman as he holds off defenders Ian Cranson and John Butler to punch a header goalwards in the 2-2 Third Division draw with Stoke on 30 November 1991. A few days later, the curtain came down on the striker's popular four-year stay at the club – comprising 63 goals in 181 appearances – when he joined Sunderland for £900,000.

Super Bob!

IT SAYS everything about Bob Taylor that Albion were prepared to pay £100,000 for him and put a three-year contract on the table less than two seasons after they had given him away for nothing! It says even more that he proceded to fully justify those apparently generous terms.

Denis Smith was the man who showed him the door, Gary Megson paid to take him back and every manager who has worked with him in his adopted Black Country has found him to be true to the Baggies cause. Bobby Gould will never go down in history as The Hawthorns' most popular boss but, among the many discoveries he has made at his various clubs, a certain £300,000 capture back in February 1992, is certainly one that will win approval and sit very comfortably even with his staunchest critics among Albion supporters.

Taylor, born in Horden in the North-East, had scored nine goals in 42 Football League games for Leeds and 50 in 106 for Bristol City when Gould signed him out of the £900,000 proceeds of Don Goodman's controversial late-1991 sale to Sunderland. The results with a club then in the Third Division were almost instant. The new boy, then a few days off his 25th birthday, scored at home to Brentford on his debut, netted twice in a 3-0 victory at promotion rivals Birmingham in his first away match and ended that third-of-a-campaign with eight goals to his credit, including one against Bolton – another club destined to play a big part in his career.

Albion's failure to reach at least a play-off place tipped Gould over the edge as far as fans were concerned, the early-1970s Hawthorns forward losing his job after supporters had carried a coffin and banners bearing RIP messages at Shrewsbury on the last day of the season. The side had beaten Preston and Shrewsbury in their final two matches of 1991-92, scoring three goals in each, but it was too little too late. There was one particularly valuable legacy, though, and Ossie Ardiles was the man who reaped the rewards. The former Tottenham and Argentinian World Cup star developed an easy-on-the-eye passing game and attacking flair that had eluded Gould and that were to provide the perfect ammunition for Taylor and, later, Andy Hunt.

Taylor went goal-crazy in 1992-93 – an elongated campaign which took Albion into the play-offs and then to Wembley glory over Midlands rivals Port Vale in the Final. He scored no fewer than 37 times in all competitions (the same tally in a single season that Fred Morris had come up with in League matches alone in 1919-20, albeit three fewer than the great W. G. Richardson's seasonal best haul of 40 in 1935-36). Taylor's total might have been even higher but, surprisingly, he didn't net any of the Baggies' six goals in the three games – against Swansea and Vale – that made up their play-off programme.

Thirty of those 1992-93 notches on the Taylor belt came in League games, including two goals against Blackpool on kick-off day and further braces against Bolton and Stoke away and Preston, Swansea and Wigan at home. The best League figures in a season by some of his counterparts in the famous blue and white striped No 9 shirt are 28 by Fred Shinton in 1906-07, 25 by George James in 1925-26, 38 by Jimmy Cookson in 1927-28, 39 by W. G. Richardson in 1935-36, 28 by Dave Walsh in 1946-47, 32 by Ronnie Allen in 1951-52 and 26 by Jeff Astle in 1967-68. Cyrille Regis's best League haul was 17 in 1981-82 and, from players in other shirts, 37 by Fred Morris in 1919-20, 28 by Johnny Nicholls in 1953-54, 24 by Bobby Robson in 1957-58, 33 by Derek Kevan in 1961-62, 28 by Tony Brown in 1970-71 and 31 by Lee Hughes in 1998-99 are the best League hauls.

Taylor topped 20 as Albion, under Keith Burkin-shaw, avoided relegation by the skin of their teeth in 1993-94 and did the same when named Hawthorns skipper in 1995-96. When that campaign under Alan Buckley ended on a high note with a placing of 11th despite an horrendous mid-winter slump, his tally for the club was exactly 100 in 228 senior appearances. All told, his Albion total of competitive goals stood at 124 come the end of the 2000-01 season. That leaves him eighth in the club's all-time marksmen list behind W. G. Richardson (328 including wartime), Tony Brown (279), Allen (234), Astle (174), Kevan (173), Joe Carter (155) and Tommy Glidden (140). And it's a tally that would have been considerably greater but for the two-year stint he had at Bolton from the spring of 1998 to just before the transfer deadline in March 2000.

Clearly, the player is still highly regarded at the Reebok Stadium and, when Megson's men slipped to defeat there in the play-offs in May 2001, he went off on his own personal salute to Bolton fans after first acclaiming Albion's 5,000-plus travelling supporters. He is one of football's true nice guys as well as a prominent figure in Albion history; intelligent on and off the field and up there with the Astles and the Regises in terms of popularity. Bob Taylor might not have been a scorer of great goals but he's certainly a great scorer of goals.

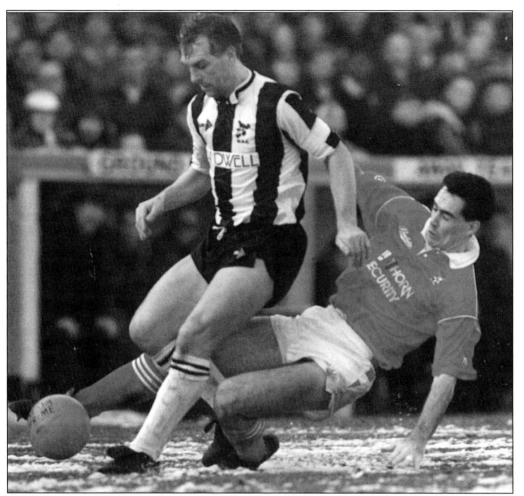

Typical aggression from Bob Taylor as he slides in, while still a Bristol City player, on Albion defender Graham Roberts in a Second Division clash at snowy Ashton Gate on 2 February 1991. Taylor scored one of the goals as the West Country outfit won 2-0 – Albion's sixth successive away defeat after they had also gone out of the League Cup on the same ground the previous August. In 1992, Taylor was an Albion player. *Picture courtesy of Bristol Evening Post.*

The best £300,000 Bobby Gould spent as Albion boss. A few months after Don Goodman's controversial £900,000 sale to Sunderland, Bob Taylor – formerly of Leeds and Bristol City – checked in at The Hawthorns at the end of January 1992. Chairman John Silk is present to witness the formalities.

'Super Bob' hails the Birmingham Road End – then still a terraced area – after netting his first Albion goal in his first appearance for them. It came on 1 February, just two days after his signing, in a 2-0 Third Division home win against Brentford.

First away game, first away goals… a week on from his debut, Taylor wheels away towards Craig Shakespeare (left) and Graham Harbey after netting one of his brace in the 3-0 victory away to promotion rivals Birmingham. The striker came to enjoy his visits to St Andrew's.

And it's goal No 4 in only his fifth outing… Taylor tucks home a low shot to provide the high spot in Albion's 2-1 defeat at Bournemouth on 22 February 1992. He was to end his first third of a season at the club with eight goals from 19 games – a sure sign of what was to come as he successfully filled the boots of the departed Don Goodman. The Bournemouth goalkeeper is Vince Bartram, who later had a loan spell with Albion.

New season, new manager, same old result… Taylor, sporting Albion's radical new strip, nets one of his two goals at home to Blackpool on the first day of 1992-93. Looking on approvingly during Ossie Ardiles's first game in charge are Gary Strodder (grounded), Bernard McNally and Simon Garner.

The finishing line was close when Albion took on Hull, wearing a garish tiger-colour strip, on the last day of the 1992-93 League programme. Taylor, tormenting his markers here, scored once and Andy Hunt twice in a 3-0 win but the Baggies had to be content with a place in the play-offs despite a five-game run-in of four victories and a draw.

All's worthwhile! Taylor celebrates with midfielder Bernard McNally during the open-top bus tour that followed Albion's play-off final victory over Port Vale at Wembley in May 1993. Strangely, the striker didn't score in the play-offs but his goal tally for the season was still a highly impressive 37 in League and cups.

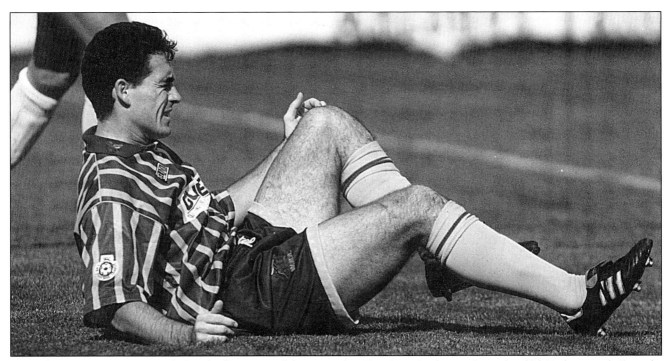

Ouch, that one hurt! A grimace during the first game of the season in 1994-95 – a 1-1 draw at Luton in which Taylor scored. Bizarrely, Albion began Keith Burkinshaw's last part-campaign with five successive away League matches because of Hawthorns building work and also crammed a League Cup first leg at Hereford into the first week of the season.

Andy Hunt (left) and Paul Raven are full of admiration as Taylor scores with a tremendous overhead kick in Albion's 1-1 home draw against Oldham on 18 January 1997 – Alan Buckley's last game before being sacked as Hawthorns boss.

Denis Smith decided the 'Super Bob' Hawthorns era was over in the spring of 1998 and packed him off on a free transfer to Bolton for a taste of the Premiership. It was a strange experience for Albion fans to see the striker in rival colours and Daryl Burgess had no wish to be too friendly when the two teams subsequently did battle at the Reebok Stadium, far left. But the man who had been a great crowd-pleaser in the Black Country showed he had a flair for good PR as well when, on another Albion visit to Bolton in mid-February 1999, left, he swapped shirts at the end with Lee Hughes and kissed the badge of his old club, much to the delight of the travelling fans.

When the chips were down in March 2000, and Albion were staring relegation in the face, new boss Gary Megson decided Taylor still had a big part to play. He signed him back for £100,000 on a three-year contract. It looked erratic business by the club but Taylor had a packed Hawthorns crowd celebrating on the final day of the season when he scored one of the goals that beat promoted Charlton 2-0 and guaranteed survival at the expense of neighbours Walsall.

Shoots of Recovery

The charge for promotion from what was now the Second Division was well and truly on when Ossie Ardiles's Albion went to Exeter on 16 January 1993. Even the Devon club's two-goal lead didn't halt the bandwagon, Carl Heggs, Gary Hackett and Ian Hamilton (penalty) scoring the second-half goals that chalked up three more points. Heggs looks on here as Darren Bradley aims a header towards the target.

Andy Hunt celebrates one of his hat-trick goals against Brighton on his Albion home debut on 3 April 1993. The striker, signed by Ossie Ardiles from Newcastle, initially on loan and then for a bargain £100,000, had also scored at Bradford in his first game for the club six days earlier. He scored nearly 90 goals in around 230 appearances for the club and, after a Bosman free transfer to Charlton, was the First Division top scorer in 1999-2000 prior to having to quit the game several months later with a mystery illness.

Central defender Gary Strodder roars his deligh[t] Ian Hamilton after the midfielder had put Albio[n] ahead on aggregate in t[he] Second Division play-off semi-final against Swans[ea] in May 1993. Trailing 2-1 from the first leg at the Vetch Field, Albion roare[d] back with goals by Andy Hunt and Hamilton on a vibrant night in front of 26,045 fans to go throu[gh] a Wembley meeting wit[h] Port Vale.

And it was joy in the final as well, where second-half goals by Andy Hunt, Nicky Reid and Kevin Donovan sunk Vale 3-0. Here, Gary Strodder pops up between Robbie Van der Laan (right) and Dean Glover to further raise the hopes of an estimated 40,000 Albion fans in a crowd of more than 53,000.

A player from the 'goal scoring greats' category – and the one on the right wasn't bad either! Lee Hughes is congratulated by England World Cup Final goalkeeper Gordon Banks and the legendary Pele as he receives a cap to mark his appearance in the England semi-professional side in 1997. The hand-over, made a week after Hughes had moved to The Hawthorns from Kidderminster for £300,000, preceded the FA Umbro Trophy Final between Dagenham and Woking.

Carefully does it... Lee Hughes keeps his head over the ball and his balance is just perfect as he sidefoots home the penalty he himself had won in the first half of the midweek Black Country derby against Wolves at The Hawthorns in October 2000. The striker was to score 23 goals in a campaign that took the club to the play-offs.

We'll Be Alright! Proud Albion fans yell their backing as Gary Megson's players are given a heart-warming send-off into the close season following their play-off semi-final second-leg defeat at Bolton on 17 May 2001. Sixth place in the First Division represented the club's highest finish in the 92 since they last dropped out of the top flight in 1986.

Subscribers

Bryan Royston Adams

Dylan John Adams

Matthew & Daniel Adams

John Aldridge

Mark Allard

Geoff Allman

David Allock

Fraser Ellis Alsop

Mr R M Anstis

Keith Archer

Nicolas Archer

Robert Arms

John A Armstrong

Robert W Arnold

Mr Gary K Ashman

Anthony Ashmore

Philip Astley

Alex Aston

Lil Aston

Scott Edward Baggott

Jonathan Bagley

John Albert Bailey

Lee Bailey

Stephen Bailey

Lisa Baker

Matthew Baker

Martin Banner

Cyril Banyard

Steve Barber

Sidney Bate

Michael Baxter

Michael Beard

Steve Beard

Ron A Beards

Ronald Beardsmore

David Beetison

Neil Bell

Fred Bellingham

Mark James Benbow

Albert Bench

John Bennett

John Benton

Thomas Bettam

Michael Billingham

Brian Bird

Mike Bisseker

Ian Blackham

Norman Blakesley

Ross Blakeway

Neil Blockley

Chris Blocksidge

Robert S Bradley

Richard Bramwell

Alan Bratt

Darren Bratt

Malcolm Bridges

Neil Brookes

John G Brown

Philip J Brown

Graham Brownhill

Mick Bryan

William Luke Buckley

Melvin Bullas

Stuart Bullock

Philip David Burgess

Geoff Burkinshaw

Ann Burton

Daniel William Burton

F A Burton

Bryan Caddick

Fred & Carol Carter

Jon Carter

Ian Cartwright

Kevin R Cashmore

Peter Cashmore

Harold Raymond Chandler

Kirsty Cherrington

Peter Chilton

Paul Clark

John Clarke

Peter Clarke

Susie Clitheroe

Steven & Jake Clorley

Darren Cooper

Trevor Collins

Dennis Corbett

James Cornfield

Philip Cornfield

Neil Dams

Mr Joseph Dangerfield

Richard T Davenport

Trevor Davenport

Kenneth Charles Davey

Bob Davies

Andrew Thomas Davies

Mike Davis

William B J Dawes

James Deakin

Martyn Derby

Nial James Devlin

John Dickinson

John Dixon

Simon Dixon

Andrew Paul Dodd

Roy Doran

Julian Dowen

Patrick Dowling

Trevor Dubberley

Vince Duddy

Steven Dudley

Martin Duke

Gary Paul Dunn

Paul East

Tony Edgington

Jon Edwards

D J Elcock

Mark Eley

Jonathan Elliott

B R Evans

Nigel Evans

Stewart Evans

Graham Evers

Christopher Farley

John Farley

Hedley Farr

Melvyn Farr

Melvyn John Farr

Paul Fellows

Simon J Fenton

Henry Coley Fisher

Robert Fisher

Stuart Fisher

Craig Fletcher

Kevin Fletcher

Christopher J Foxall

Alan Graham Franks

Dave Fryer

Maurice Gaunt

Major Singh Ghuman

Stuart Gibbons

Terry Gibbons

Ian Ashley Gibbs

Kieron Gibson

Roger Gilbert

I D Glen

Tony Golcher

A S Goodall

Maurice Goodwin

Nathan Gorrod

Julia Gough

Ian Goulcher

Edward Gould

Douglas Graham

James R Grainger

Richard Grainger

Steven Grainger

Terry Grainger

David Granby

Lee Gray

Alan Green

John Green

Peter Winston Green

Sophie Kirsty Green

Darren Gregg

Graham Grice

Peter Griffin

Robert A Griffiths

David Grigg

Wayne Grigg

Peter Grimley

Robert Hale

Ben Hall

Bill Hardy

Robin H Harman

George Christian Harmon

M D Harper

Delroy Harris

Marc Harris

Nicholas Harrold

Paul Hart

Norman John Hartshorne

David Harvey

John Hawker

Godfrey 'Grandpa' Hawkins

Keith Hazelhurst

Matthew Hennefer

Alan Hingley

Mark Hipkiss

Ivor J Hodgetts

David Hollingmode

James Holmes

Stuart Holmes

Michael & Matthew Holton

Ian Robert Homer

Mr Joseph Anthony Homer

Robert Hooper

Brian Horton

Mark Horton

Zoe Horton

Ian Hoult

Mr Barry Hughes

Elliott Hughes

Mr J F Hughes

Lawson Hunt

Stuart Hunt

Simon Husselbee

Terry Ingram

Graham Jackson

Gary James

Ron Jarratt

S M & L M Jeens

Ian Jenkins

Richard Jenkins

Alan Jennings

Alexander Johnson

Andrew Jones

Aubrey Jones

Brendan Jones

Craig Jones

Eddie V Jones

Phil Jones

Simon Jones

Trefor Jones

Leslie Kenny

Gary Kidney

Arthur B Lawford

Dennis Lawley

Ray Lawrence

Graham Lawton

Wilfred R Layland

Lee

Bob Lee

Jason Douglas Lee

Stephen Lee

Marina Leese

Gary Lewis

Jayne Lightwood

Simon Lissemore

Michelle Lyons

Patrick McAlister

Timothy McCarthy

Clive McDermott

Marcus McDermott

Gareth McDonald

Eamonn McGeough

S G McNeil

Cathy & John Maddox

Tony Maher

Zenon Malinowski

Paul Malley

Lee Manning

Liam Marshall

Jordan Martin

Kevin Martin

Freda Matthews

Liam Philip Matthews

Arron K Meeson

Vanessa & Fawne Melia

Vanessa Melia

Philip Millard

Ashley Millinchip

Leonard Millington

Billy T Mills

Mick Mills

Neville E J Mills

Paul Mills

Robert L Mills

Ron Mills

Samuel John Mills

Stephen J Mills

Helen Moore

June Moore

Chas Morris

Lee Morton

Craig Moseley

Martin Moseley

Paul Moseley

Sarah Moseley

Stuart R Mowat

Ian Munro

Frank Nagy

Geoff Nevey

Les Newman

Tom Nicholls

Kevin Nichols

Richard Noake

Chris Nock

Trevor Norris

Daniel & Andy Norton

Josh Owen

Royston Paddock

Kevin Page

Steven John Palmer

Linda Palmer

Ellen Marie Parton

John Payton

Jonathon A Pearson

Iain Perrins

Jeffrey Perry

David A Phillips

Mike Phipps

Christopher Pickering

Les Pike

Alan Pittaway

James Plant

Samuel Plant

Carl Poulton

Matthew J Powell

Mike Priddy

Glen Priest

Chris Pritchard

Darren Probert

Michael Proctor

Cyril Randle

Richard Randle

M J F Reaney

Mark Andrew Reed

Jonathan Reid

Paul Rich

Daniel & Simon Richards

Christine Riley

Andy Roberts

Eric Roberts

Paul Roberts

David Rogers

Malcolm Rose

Michael Ian Ross

Jonathan Clive Round

Julian Rowe

Gary Roy

John F Rudge

Geoff Rushton

Carl Ruston

Joseph Ryan

Brian Sambrooks

James Thomas Saunders

Geoff Sedgley

Mark E Selwood

Alan Sheppard

Barry Shermer

John Sidaway

Judy Simcox

Bob Skelding

John T Skidmore

James Slater

Andy Sloan

Derek Smart

Bradley Thomas Smith

Clive William Smith

David Smith

James Smith

Neil Smith

Steven Sorrill

Colin Southall

Mitch Southall

Paul Spence

David Spicer

Martyn Spink

C J Spruce

James B Stanistreet

Paul Barry Steventon

Frank Stockley

Ken Stockton

David Stokes

Lee Stokes

Paul Stokes

Stan Sunley

Nick Sulivan

David J Taylor

David Vincent Taylor

Laurie D Taylor

Leigh Taylor

Mrs Edna Taylor

Jonathan Tedstone

Mike Teece

Mr Alfred W Thomas

Michael Thomas

Christopher Tilley

A J Timmins

Simon M Tracey

Jonathan Joseph Tranter

Brian Trevis

Peter Turner

Roger Turner

Steven Turner

Tony Turner

Pauline Tyler

Mr E G Vaughan

Brett Andrew Wain

Bill Waite

Malcolm Waite

Geoff Walker

Terence Neil Wall

Sean Wallader

Colin Walter

Stephen Walter

Mr B P Walters

Jonathan Peter Want

David Warner

Warren & Aiden

Mike Warren

Barry Micheal Watson

Steve Watton

Jamie Wheatley

Andrew White

Dr Andrew M Whitehouse

Derek Whitehouse

Geoff & Andy Whitehouse

Kelvin Elson-Whittaker

Kevin G Whittingham

Colin J Winchurch

Jonathan Winwood

Lee Williams

Paul N Williams

Stephen Williams

Warren Wilson

Tony Witts

Huw Wiseman

Alan G Wood

Darrell Wood

Les H Woodhall

Mr A R Worley

Mrs B Wright

David Yarnall

Mrs Jean Zoeller